Praise for *Illuminating Our True Nature*

"The demand for healing tools has never been greater in these critical times. *Illuminating Our True Nature* provides a comprehensive framework for connecting with ourselves through yoga. This profound work guides us toward personal healing and illuminates a path toward healing on a collective level, making it an essential resource for our current moment."

—Dianne Bondy, author of *Yoga Where You Are*

"Through her deep philosophical study and sharing of vulnerable lived experiences, Michelle Johnson offers meaningful tools for understanding and navigating the *kleshas*, afflictions that cause suffering, while steering the reader back to the path toward liberation."

—Tejal Patel, yoga teacher, podcaster, community organizer

"With remarkable generosity, Michelle Johnson equips us with the essential tools to take deliberate and compassionate action, facilitating positive change not only within ourselves but also within our communities and the broader world. This is an important book that should be read by anyone seeking liberation and desiring that same liberation for all."

—Seane Corn, author of *Revolution of the Soul*

"In this immediately useful book, Michelle serves as a compassionate guide to help you alleviate your personal suffering. When you do that work, you can then remove obstacles to our collective liberation. Her approachable writing explains what could be opaque and inaccessible in clear language that will directly help you to help yourself—and everyone around you."

—Sage Rountree, PhD, E-RYT500, author of
The Art of Yoga Sequencing and *Teaching Yoga Beyond the Poses*

"Michelle Cassandra Johnson offers a powerful and unique perspective on the kleshas—five poisons rooted in ignorance that obscure the mind and close the heart. She asks us to consider not only how they cause suffering in our own lives but how they contribute to systems of oppression. Her wise and compassionate counsel, coupled with practices of deep reflection, is the medicine we need to bring us home to our true nature and, in doing so, work toward the liberation of all beings."

—Linda Sparrowe, author of
The Woman's Book of Yoga and Health and *Yoga Mama*

Illuminating Our True Nature

Yogic Practices for Personal
and Collective Healing

Michelle Cassandra Johnson

SHAMBHALA

Shambhala Publications, Inc.
2129 13th Street
Boulder, Colorado 80302
www.shambhala.com

Cover design: Daniel Urban-Brown
Interior design: Gopa & Ted2, Inc

9 8 7 6 5 4 3 2 1

First Edition
Printed in the United States of America

Shambhala Publications makes every effort to print
on acid-free, recycled paper.
Shambhala Publications is distributed worldwide by
Penguin Random House, Inc., and its subsidiaries.

Library of Congress Cataloging-in-Publication Data
Names: Johnson, Michelle (Michelle Cassandra), author.
Title: Illuminating our true nature: yogic practices for personal and
collective healing / Michelle Cassandra Johnson.
Description: First edition. | Boulder, Colorado: Shambhala Publications,
[2024] | Includes bibliographical references.
Identifiers: LCCN 2023027912 | ISBN 9781645471875 (trade paperback)
Subjects: LCSH: Yoga.
Classification: LCC B132.Y6 J617 2024 | DDC 613.7/046–dc23/
eng/20231128
LC record available at https://lccn.loc.gov/2023027912

Contents

Foreword

THE SUMMER OF 2020 is deeply etched in my memory. The summer of civic unrest and nationwide protests, people uprising the world over for justice, for Black liberation. I was searching, seeking, praying, looking for answers. I had many questions, much to unpack, unravel, and unlearn about the country I had come to as a starry-eyed immigrant from India. How do I show up as a brown woman? How can I serve this moment of racial reckoning as a Yoga practitioner? How can the teachings and the practices of my ancestors support and heal this wounded world we live in? I found a book called *Skill in Action: Radicalizing Your Yoga Practice to Create a Just World* by Michelle Cassandra Johnson. Michelle's words gave wings to a dream, to many dreams, of practicing the teachings of Yoga in the times we live in. Since then, I have studied with her in her Race and Resilience programs, worked with her in different capacities as a colleague, and been a guest teacher in her offerings. It has been a true honor to be in community with her.

Michelle's work invites us to practice the teachings of Yoga unflinchingly as skillful, courageous, and compassionate action, to examine the tenets as an anchor for self- and collective transformation. We cannot turn away from the overwhelm about the future of the planet. We cannot deny the threat posed by unbridled human consumption. We cannot bypass the impact of colonization that continues to manifest in our institutional and systemic DNA. We cannot afford to be silent when body autonomy is negated by draconian laws over reproductive rights and relentless attack on trans rights. Authoritarian governments, neofascism, and religious fundamentalism are on the rise all over the world. There is a sharpened polarization based on political ideologies and economic disparities. More than ever, we are in need of solace and healing of intergenerational and historic trauma. More than ever, we need practices that will hold us and offer succor as we learn, unlearn, and unravel our individualistic *samskaras*, metabolize our grief, shame, guilt, and anger. More than ever, we need to peel away the layers of our ignorance and reveal our undeniable interconnectedness. More than ever, we need the steadfastness of people devoted to collective care. More than ever, we need the liberatory teachings of Yoga to shine a light on our deeply entrenched cultural conditioning, our socialized biases about those who are different from us.

There is much ignorance, denial, and erasure of the expansiveness of Yoga in Dominant Culture. Yoga is perceived and practiced mainly as a fitness modality. However, Yoga is a multidimensional system of techniques, paradigms, tenets, traditions, and lineages delving into the complexities of the human experience. The teachings explore our innate yearning and potential for liberation from *samsara*, the cyclicality of creation, sustenance, and destruction. One of the core teachings of Yoga is that pain (*dukkha*) is inevitable in the human experience. Each of us is unique, and yet we are all the same. We may come from diverse backgrounds, speak different languages, have varied lived experiences, and yet we all seek a release from that which causes us pain. The practice of Yoga cultivates discernment, *viveka*, into the myriad causes of our suffering and reveals our intuitive wisdom, *buddhi*.

The teachings from the Upanishads, Bhagavad Gita, and Patanjali's Yoga Sutras have influenced, inspired, and informed many social change movements. The Yoga Sutras have been at the center of many periods in human history when there was a dire need for social change and collective transformation. From ancient Arab Muslim court ministers to Buddhist and Jain scholars, from Hindu anticolonial revolutionaries to European Indophiles, the Yoga Sutras have offered solace and quenched the deep-rooted human thirst to know and uproot the causes of our suffering.

Swami Vivekananda, the charismatic orator, philosopher, and social reformer, toured the United States in 1893 articulating the esoteric wisdom of the Upanishads, the Gita, and the Sutras. His lectures were published in his classic book *Raja Yoga* in 1895, in which there was a transcription of his commentary on the Yoga Sutras. As this was the first English-language commentary, it was a turning point in the history of the Sutras, which had gone into obscurity for multiple reasons in India. Vivekananda's revival not only galvanized Indians in India with an effervescent national pride in the spiritual heritage of their ancestors, it also drew international recognition and curiosity about the practice of Yoga as a gateway for self-transformation.

The Yoga Sutras is considered the quintessential text for Yoga practitioners, as it offers "secular" systematic insight into means through which a seeker can be on a path to *moksha*, liberation. The Yoga Sutras are informed by Dualistic philosophy, or *Dvaita*, which posits that there is pure consciousness, or an ultimate, unchanging reality or consciousness, which is called *Ishvara* by Patanjali (it is also called *purusha* in Sankhya philosophy, which is very closely related to the Yoga philosophy of the Sutras). We are infused with this consciousness that is immutable, unmeasurable, and omnipresent. Then there is *prakriti*, manifest nature or primordial matter. All of tangible and subtle matter is prakriti and is subject to the laws of creation and dissolution. Prakriti is diverse, everchanging, and impermanent. The goal of Yoga is to realize that we are in essence consciousness/spirit/immortal. We are whole. We are complete. It is our attachment to prakriti that causes us dukkha.

There are fewer than four verbs in the Yoga Sutras, and yet this esoteric composition attributed to Patanjali is packed with action. We are guided with a firm and gentle hand toward the goal of enlightenment, our true nature that is Divine and Whole. The aphorisms are terse and obscure, and hence there is an imperative to study the text through commentary. This soteriological goal of Sutras is methodically addressed by ancient and modern commentators.

Illuminating Our True Nature invites us to reflect on the *kleshas*, afflictions, as points of inquiry into the causes of dukkha, suffering. Michelle offers powerful reflections that illuminate how these afflictions manifest in our personal lives *and* are the building blocks of harmful systems and institutions. The book skillfully weaves ways in which the kleshas form and shape the world we live in and offers antidotes to transform and metabolize reflections, so we can embody the teachings in our everyday lives. There is a refreshing directness in the work that compels us to unravel our deeply embedded conditioning so we can be in right relationships with each other and the planet we call home.

To embody the teachings of Yoga with dedication is not for the faint of heart, nor is it a straight line. We encounter a wild path strewn with obstacles within our minds, our psyches. We need to sort through a quagmire of samskaras that drives a wedge of separation between us. These samskaras build false and harmful social stratifications based on race, class, gender, ability, and caste. This book is an enlightening resource, as it shines an unwavering light onto the internalized and manifested obstacles, offering a needed framework for reconciliation, reconnection, and remembrance of our inherent interconnectedness.

May this work light up our paths so we may go forth with *shraddha*, dedication in our quest for liberation. May we boldly envision and co-create spaces of care. May we dedicate ourselves to heal the brokenness of the world around and within us. May we be at ease in our differences. May we witness each other's magic. May we hold the other's humanity with tenderness. May we courageously confront harm as it happens. May we love each other fiercely, and may that love translate into action.

—Anjali Rao, teacher, intersectional health
advocate, and activist

Acknowledgments

FIRST AND FOREMOST, I want to acknowledge and honor the ancient practice of yoga. I bow in deep gratitude to the ancient ones who created a holistic system based on the absolute truth that we are interconnected to all things, time, and space. Thank you to my teachers, not only the teachers who have met me on this path of yoga in physical form and translated teachings from their various backgrounds and lineages to me but also to the texts, the Yoga Sutras, the Bhagavad Gita, and all of the other inspiring ways the teachings of yoga have been shared with me. Thank you to *Skill in Action: Radicalizing Your Yoga Practice to Create a Just World*. As a book and body of work channeled through me, you opened an opportunity for me to teach from my heart and transform the wellness industry. You opened a door for me to study the path of yoga more deeply. You led me to so many beautiful humans who share the same interest as I do—to actively decrease the suffering on and to our planet.

Thank you to my editor, Beth Frankl. This is a long overdue thank-you for seeing my magic right away and for this particular project, asking me to channel my magic in a specific way. I am not sure I ever would have written about the *kleshas* without you prompting me to do so over green tea and tofu *saganaki*. Thank you for being a light, truth teller, star, guide, and friend. Much love, and may we weave magic in many ways in the future.

Thank you to my friend, Tejal Patel, who wisely told me that it was going to be interesting for me to write about the kleshas. She indicated (using different words than the ones written in this note of acknowledgment) that I would be confronted by each klesha as I wrote about it. She was right. Her wisdom was medicine, and at points when I wanted to stop writing this book, I thought of her because yoga is a confrontative practice. It asks us to see ourselves wholly, accept who we are, and change at the same time. Tejal, you may not know how your words struck me when I shared about this project with you, but they did to the core.

Thank you to Tristan Katz. You have been on this path with me for quite some time. You have always supported me. You have shared with me when what I have written has touched your heart in some way. You have believed in me, and my magic, and celebrated me countless times. I cannot wait to celebrate you more. I cannot wait to hold your future book in my hands and bless it. You are magic. Please always remember you are magic.

As always, thank you to my ancestors. This book wasn't easy to write, and your constant abiding love and support gave me everything I needed to continue to write and believe in myself as I did. Thank you for believing in me. Thank you for resourcing me. Thank you for channeling through me.

Thank you to my mother, Clara. Mom, I've written so many of these acknowledgments now, but the value of each one written about you never decreases. You are my light. You are my heart. I am because you are. Thank you for talking about God with me. Thank you for understanding we talk about God in different ways, you from the Bible and Christianity and me from yoga philosophy, Buddhism, paganism, and the Hindu pantheon. Thank you for understanding that when I meditate, I am praying, and when I strive to live my yoga, I do so in a prayerful way. Thank you for teaching me about practice and devotion. Thank you for being the kindest person I know. Thank you for breathing. Thank you for being. You, my dear, are everything.

Thank you to Charles, my husband, partner, friend, playmate, lover, and firekeeper. Thank you for listening when I told you I was writing about the reasons why we suffer. Thank you for encouraging me to continue to look at the ways we suffer. Thank you for praying for the end of suffering in your own way. Thank you for bringing me joy and laughter. Your silliness is the levity I am drawn to and need because, so often, what I am working on or writing about is so serious. Thank you for always believing I can do whatever I put my mind to. Thank you for being you.

Thank you to my best friend, Amy. You are my soul sister. Always and forever. Even though you had no idea what I was talking about when I mentioned the kleshas, you offered to listen to my musings about them as a sounding board and support person. Thanks for believing in me and calling in all the good things with and for me. I love you because you are part of what makes the experience of being human more bearable, fun, and beautiful. Besties forever!

Thank you to Jasper. Oh, Jasper. You are the most magical familiar I get to spend time with. Thank you for sitting next to me during my morning meditation and calling in all of the words for my writing projects. Thanks for letting me know when to take breaks to get outside and feel the air. Thank you for cuddling up next to me as I wrote. Thank you for protecting me and loving me so deeply. Thank you for being here now. I love you, sweet being. I love you.

Thank you to all who have supported this and past writing projects, yoga workshops, retreats, teachings, and musings. Thank you for being part of a vast web of people who desire to create a liberated world for all. We are always held by a much wider web than we think, and I am grateful to be held by you all, those in my web who are known to me and unknown in such a profound and stunning way.

Introduction

A Particular Kind of Sensitivity

Someone who is searching for clarity becomes sensitive because
the eyes must be open, even if what they see is sometimes very
unpleasant. Someone who is searching feels or sees things long
before other people do. He or she develops a special insight,
a particular kind of sensitivity. We would see this positively—this
insight or sensitivity can be as useful as a warning light in a car.
It tells us that there is something wrong and we would be wise
to find out what it is. Someone who is searching for clarity always
sees more suffering than someone who is not.
—SRI T. K. V. DESIKACHAR, *THE HEART OF YOGA*

MY MOTHER AND I were driving across the James River Bridge
in our 1970 blue Datsun station wagon. We crossed over the
bridge and were about to head down near the river en route
to our home. I looked over at my mom and said, "I don't want to have
children." Puzzled, she looked at me and asked, "Why are you thinking
about that now, Michelle?" I replied, "This world doesn't make sense to
me, and I don't want to bring a child into it. The world is violent, and I
don't want to bring a child into it." She said, "Okay, Michelle. You do not
have to decide this now. You do not have to decide this right now." We
drove the rest of the way home in silence.

I was under the age of ten when I told my mother about my decision
to not have children, and looking back, I know that many ten-year-olds
may not have been seriously thinking about their futures or the state of

the world, but I was. I thought about it all of the time. I was a sensitive child. Sensitive to energies, emotions, and the ways of the world that didn't make any sense to me. I knew suffering was real and that I was suffering, as were others. I didn't want to bring children into a world where they would suffer, and I don't think I understood how other people could continue to bring other beings into a world that was full of suffering.

This line of thinking was not only influenced by my empathic nature and pensive personality. My brother was adopted, and I knew that, on some level, the suffering I experienced was different from his. His birth family had given him up, and mine had not. I imagined he longed to know more about where he was from, even though he seemed content with where he had ended up—with us, me and my mother. The tears my mother would allow to run down her face late at night when she thought we were sleeping let me know she was suffering, too. My father had left us, and even though he was no longer physically in our home, the ghost of him was everywhere, and the way he haunted my mother made her suffer. I knew my grandfather, Fred, was also suffering. He would hide out in his room, drink whiskey, and want to be left alone. I think he was trying to find some peace in a world that felt anything but peaceful to him. I knew that the children my mother taught in her special education classes were suffering, too. My mother would take me on home visits with her, and I saw, firsthand, environments where parents who have been neglected repeat the cycle of neglect with their children in turn. I remember these families not having enough food, safe and clean shelter, and stability within their homes.

I was suffering, too. I was the only Black girl in my class in elementary school. I felt isolated and alone and knew that the way I was suffering—because of an educational system that didn't value Black bodies—was different from my friend Alison's experience as a white-bodied girl. Though she suffered, too—her parents worked all of the time, and she felt neglected and unseen—still, her suffering felt different from mine.

As I grew older, my questions about the nature of suffering didn't decrease. In fact, my curiosity increased so much that, at times, all I could see and feel was the suffering, which didn't allow me to notice what else was present in my life or the world. When I was fourteen, I was hospitalized in a psychiatric ward for a month. Looking back now, I think all the suffering I had witnessed, was aware of, and had experienced up until that point felt so overwhelming that I didn't feel like I could be in my body anymore. I am not sure I was really suicidal. I don't think so, but I didn't have any other way to describe how I was feeling other than stating to my psychiatrist that I wanted to die. What I really believe I wanted to convey is that I wanted all of the suffering inside me and in our world to stop.

When I went to college, my awareness of suffering continued. I watched one of my friends having to fight an institution that was hell-bent on defaming her after she came forward to tell her story of being sexually assaulted by a group who were part of a fraternity known for that kind of behavior. I sat with her for hours over the course of a year and listened to all the dirty tactics the college used to try to keep her silent and, really, to make her go away. Eventually, she did.

After college, I went to graduate school to become a clinical social worker. In so many ways, it made sense that I decided to train to sit with and support people as they move through their suffering. The entire field of social work originated from a desire to decrease the injustice that exists in our world—injustice emerging from the pattern of suffering we have created and continue to perpetuate for ourselves and others.

While I was in graduate school, I was introduced to Hatha Yoga. At first, I was mainly practicing *asana,* and then a teacher introduced me to yoga philosophy by reading from texts such as the Yoga Sutras in his classes. My interest in yoga and learning more about the eight-limbed path was piqued, and I came to believe the practice of yoga might be a pathway for us as a collective to turn toward our suffering, better understand it, and mitigate future suffering. I believed the pathway of yoga might not only help us better understand suffering but also support us in creating conditions for justice in our world. My interest in yoga turned into a more profound devotion to the practice and path of yoga, which eventually led to me deepening my study of yoga by attending 200-hour and 300-hour yoga teacher trainings, followed by many other trainings over the past fourteen years. Throughout this time, most of my yoga practice has been explicitly rooted in better understanding and teaching about the intersection of yoga and justice, and how to radicalize the practice of yoga to create a just world. This aligns with what yoga teaches us—to remove obstacles that are in the way of us experiencing *samadhi*, liberation.

My study of yoga has included the study of the Yoga Sutras, the Bhagavad Gita, and other sacred yogic texts. These sacred yogic texts have taken time for me to digest, and I continue to study and deepen my understanding of the content offered in them. I strive to apply the teachings to my own lived experience and the current cultural context. The Yoga Sutras are said to have originated from a man named Patanjali and throughout time have been translated by many teachers and scholars. The root word *sutra* comes from the same root as the medical term *suture*—*sutra* means thread. The 196 sutras are threaded together to provide a map of how to live a peaceful and happy life.

Book Two of the Yoga Sutras, the Sadhana Pada, teaches that there are five afflictions that cause us to suffer. These are called the *kleshas*. The five kleshas are *avidya* (ignorance), *asmita* (overidentification with the ego), *raga* (attachment to pleasure or desire), *dvesha* (avoidance), and *abhinivesha* (fear of death and letting go). After introducing the afflictions, or kleshas, the Sadhana Pada explores how the kleshas lead us to develop *samskaras* (patterns or tendencies) and how our samskaras lead to our *karma* (consequences). The chapter teaches that the path of Ashtanga, or the eight-limbed path, is our way to decrease our suffering.

Through my study of the Yoga Sutras, and Book Two in particular, I began to think back to how sensitive to suffering I was as a child. I began to feel how sensitive I continue to be in response to the suffering we experience and create in this world. I started to consider how the yogic pathway, a pathway rooted in liberation, at a minimum could decrease our suffering and, at a maximum, could allow us to shift our relationship with suffering in a way that will enable us to be free. I started to ponder how we might better understand the causes and impact of our ignorance, willful or unwillful; overidentification with the ego and our identities; attachment to pleasure; pattern of avoiding and bypassing the relative truth; and our fear of death and of letting go. I began to wonder how we could work to break or interrupt patterns and tendencies that cause more suffering due to the consequences of our actions, or karma.

I began to become curious about how we could engage the path of yoga to reset the karmic path of the collective.

We are suffering in many ways right now. We have been living with a virus, COVID-19, that has mutated multiple times and still plagues us. We are grieving the loss of many people due to this virus. We are living during a time when fault lines in the foundations of institutions such as housing, banking, agriculture, education, social services, healthcare, and the like are being revealed more clearly. We are living in a political and cultural climate riddled with upheaval. We are reckoning with the systems of white supremacy, patriarchy, capitalism, and a fragile economic system. We are living in colonized bodies, and our sovereignty continues to be taken away by a dominant culture enacting oppression through policies put in place to control our bodies. We are living with colonized minds that lead us to believe our individual care is more important than collective care.

We are experiencing record-breaking temperatures across the globe because of what humans have done to the climate and our ecosystems. Senseless wars are being waged. We are experiencing polarization within ourselves and our communities. We are suffering because we believe we are separate from one another rather than understanding we are wholly and completely interdependent and interconnected. Suffering is in the DNA housed in our bodies. It has been passed on to us. It is part of what we have inherited from our ancestors, and the legacies left to us from toxic systems wedded to dominance, power-over, and the idea that some beings are supreme and others are disposable.

Although the aforementioned suffering is both part of what we have inherited and part of what we perpetuate, and while suffering is in our genetic and physical DNA—literally passed on from one generation to the next—suffering is not inherent to our true nature. The kleshas take root because of our inability to remember our true nature and connection with all beings. Yoga, as a pathway and practice, suggests that we can work toward discovering our true nature and the nature of all things. We are in an intricate and intimate relationship with everyone and everything; working toward uncovering our true nature brings us into union with all beings, thus decreasing our suffering.

Illuminating Our True Nature: Yogic Practices for Personal and Collective Healing is intended to provide an understanding of how the kleshas originate from the belief we are separate from one another and the planet. The content and practices offered throughout this book are intended to provide the reader with more knowledge about how each specific klesha causes suffering for us as individuals and the collective, and how the kleshas lead us to create tendencies and karma that move us away from realizing and remembering our true nature. This leads to a constant cycle of suffering for us all. The book explores how the removal of obstacles mitigates suffering and creates new tendencies and ways of being that will create consequences (karma) that allow us to build a world in which we can all come into our true nature and experience freedom. *Illuminating Our True Nature* is broken down into five sections, one on each klesha. Each section includes three short chapters about that klesha and concludes with an *asana pranayama*, meditation, *mudra*, and mantra practice as well. Many of the chapters also include reflection questions.

Illuminating Our True Nature: Yogic Practices for Personal and Collective Healing is a guide for how we can turn toward, instead of move away from, our suffering, not only to better understand why we suffer but also to open up pathways to freedom. As you engage with this book, it is my hope that you learn to decrease your own suffering—not just for yourself but for us all, so that we all will suffer less and learn to understand the ways in which we each have a role to play in building a world that is ultimately free of suffering.

I want to take a moment to locate myself. I am a Black, cisgender person who has been socialized as a female. I am heterosexual, although not really wedded to this identity. I am unsure of how to identify myself regarding my sexual orientation, and I am currently in a heterosexual relationship. I am an American citizen. I am middle class. I own my home. I have an advanced degree. I am not currently experiencing a physical or mental disability. I struggle with depression at times. Each one of the identities I am listing informs my experience of my inner world and the outer world, including how I ingest and digest the teachings of yoga.

In this book, I offer my perspective on the Yoga Sutras and the nature of our suffering, and ideas about how to remove obstacles so we suffer less and find freedom. My perspective has been shaped by my experience in the world, which has been shaped by the identities I embody and the path of yoga. Up until a few years ago, the majority of my yoga teachers were white, cisgender women. Both my 200-hour and my 300-hour yoga teacher trainings were taught predominantly by white-bodied people.

I learned the lineage of Ashtanga yoga through a white lens, and I imagine my formative experiences of learning about yoga would have been different had I been taught predominantly by South Asian yoga practitioners and teachers and by Black, Indigenous, and People of Color practitioners and teachers. I have taken the teachings of yoga and tried to understand how they fit into my life. I understand the interpretations I offer in this book are interpretations that have been shaped by my identities and lived experience and also by who taught me the lessons of yoga and how they taught me through their own various lenses. I am sharing this here because it feels important to name that I have taken the teachings of Patanjali out of context.

I wasn't alive when Patanjali was. I am not South Asian. I have not learned lessons in the way Patanjali would have taught them, chanting one sutra at a time. This means it is likely I will miss something or interpret teachings in ways that may not match your understanding of the Yoga Sutras, kleshas, samskaras, and karma, especially if you are South Asian and on the path of yoga. If you are not South Asian and haven't been handed down the lineage of yoga from South Asian teachers, my understanding of the concepts offered in this book still may not match your understanding or experience of yoga. I ask that you read and work with the offerings in this book. I ask that you learn what you can from what I have to offer. It is my hope I have offered my understanding of the path of yoga with humility and curiosity. This is part of what the path has taught me, how to be humble and curious. I mean no harm and hope I am as reverent as one can be, because I believe in the path of yoga, and I trust it has the tools we need to heal and repair the things that feel so broken in our world. I trust the path of yoga and commit to it wholeheartedly.

My words above bring this Shanti mantra to mind:

OṀ SAHA NĀVAVATU
SAHA NAU BHUNAKTU
SAHA VĪRYAṀ KARAVĀVAHAI
TEJASVI NĀVADHĪTAMASTU MĀ VIDVIṢĀVAHAI
OṀ ŚĀNTIḤ ŚĀNTIḤ ŚĀNTIḤ

Om, may we be protected.
May we be nourished.
May we work together with great vigor.
May our intellect be sharpened and our study be effective.
Let there be no animosity between us.
Om peace (in me), peace (in nature), peace (in divine forces).

May this book be offered in the spirit of this chant.

Essential Tools for Our Journey

To begin our journey in *Illuminating Our True Nature* together, you will want to gather a few essential tools.

1. Review the following sections on Shared Language and Approach and Assumptions to familiarize yourself with the language presented this book.

2. Get a journal for recording reflections as you move through this book. This journal will serve as a space for you to record your thoughts, feelings, awakenings, and ideas.

3. I invite you to create a sacred space in your home, car, or office or in a natural landscape (such as a favorite park, hillside, river, or stream) to practice the asana, pranayama, mantra, and mudra practices. You will want to have pillows, blankets, a mat, and/or any other items you need to practice these offerings fully.

4. Last, I encourage you to find an object that represents both suffering and liberation, or two objects—one representative of suffering and one representative of liberation. Choose an object or objects that are meaningful to you. Place your object(s) in a location where

you will see them daily to remind you of the importance of better understanding why we suffer and of our pathway to freedom.

Shared Language

Offering shared language is a way to support you, the reader, in better understanding the context in which I—and we—exist and in better understanding my perspective. In this book I may use terminology that is new to you or used in a different way than you are accustomed to. Many of the definitions offered here are informed by my work with Dismantling Racism Works (dRWorks), *Skill in Action: Radicalizing Your Yoga Practice to Create a Just World,* and critical race and feminist theory.

Culture
Norms, standards, beliefs, values, and narratives created and maintained by a particular nation, people, or social group.

Dominant Culture
Dominant culture is a system that inherently believes some people are superior and others inferior. This system of dominance and inferiority is based on various identities, such as race, gender identity and expression, age, physical and mental capabilities, and sexual orientation. Dominant culture creates norms, thus deeming who is "normal." When one is seen as normal based on their identities, this gives them closer proximity to power. Therefore, dominant culture functions as a gatekeeper by deciding who has access to power and, furthermore, access to moving with ease as they navigate their life.

Social Location
Social location refers to one's social group membership and identities. It is a tool used to reflect on the groups you belong to because of your place or position in history and society. It is a tool you can use to clearly identify your proximity to power based on identities you embody. All of us have a social location that is defined by race, gender and gender expression, social class, age, ability level, sexual orientation, geographic location, and context.

Cultural Trauma

Cultural trauma is a dysregulation of the collective's nervous system, often due to systemic oppression and in response to tragic and horrific events that forever shift a group of people's consciousness and identity. Cultural trauma acknowledges the shared experience of trauma even as people respond to the traumatic event(s) differently.

Suffering

So much of what will be explored in *Illuminating Our True Nature* is about the nature and causes of our individual and collective suffering. Given the historical legacy of war, violence, oppression, socially and politically constructed categories that minimize some people and make them be seen as subhuman, and the privileging of certain groups of people at the expense of others, it is important to understand the ways we are suffering individually and how our individual suffering is connected to our collective suffering. Suffering is the experience of pain and distress psychically, emotionally, physically, mentally, and spiritually. Systems of supremacy such as white supremacy, patriarchy, capitalism, colonialism, and xenophobia are founded on the belief that some people deserve to feel pain and experience distress psychically, emotionally, physically, mentally, and spiritually.

Yoga

I could offer a very long definition, because yoga is something I continue to study and my understanding of it evolves over time. For the purposes of this section, we can understand yoga as meaning to "yoke," or come into union. Often I think about the process of coming into union as coming into alignment with oneself and all things. The practice of yoga is intended to support us in coming back to our true nature and essence, which at times people describe as love, light, liberation, or connection to all that has been, is now, and will be.

Spiritual Bypassing

Spiritual bypassing is a term coined by John Welwood. He defined spiritual bypassing as "spiritual ideas and practices to sidestep personal, emotional 'unfinished business,' to shore up a shaky sense of self, or to belittle basic needs, feelings, and developmental tasks."[1] Spiritual bypassing arises in many spiritual spaces, which causes great harm to us all. An example of this is the statement, "We are one." This belief is a tenant of many spiritual practices and religions and is an absolute truth, and yet we live in a culture where we are not able to live as one due to systemic oppression. We are not having the same experience, based on our different identities, social location, and proximity to power. A valuable practice is being able to hold an absolute truth while holding the reality of what is happening that moves us away from that truth. We cannot bypass our individual or collective suffering, and many spiritual communities of which I've been a part have focused on enlightenment or transcendence as the goal, which hasn't forced them to reckon with the reasons why we suffer collectively or to heal the cultural trauma we experience.

Liberation

As with the definition of suffering, many religious and faith traditions, including Buddhism and Hinduism, focus on the pathway to enlightenment as a process of freeing ourselves of our attachments to afflictions (our own suffering) and shifting our consciousness such that we can be free regardless of the circumstances. I would describe liberation as freedom and ease. Liberation is also deeply connected to the rights one is given or the rights that are taken away based on one's social location and proximity to power.

Spirit/Divine/God

I conceptualize "Spirit" as a power and energy that is much larger than and contained inside me. Spirit can be felt through the elements—air, water, on the earth, in the heavens, in our bodies, and around us. People use different words to describe Spirit, including God, Father, Creator, Divine, Mother, and others. Spirit is an energy from which I seek guidance and support. I pray to Spirit, and my spirit guides each day. Spirit guides are energies in the spiritual, not material, world who are positive in nature and offer assistance to me in various ways. Spirit guides are sometimes referred to as angels, archangels, guardians, elemental energies, and ancestors.

Approach and Assumptions

As I write *Illuminating Our True Nature,* I am not neutral. I have a particular perspective about why we suffer and the cause of our suffering. Here, I offer a list of assumptions as a way of being transparent about my lack of neutrality. The practice of offering assumptions derived from a collaboration with my colleagues at Dismantling Racism Works (dRWorks). Assumptions speak further to beliefs, values, and the historical and current cultural and political context. Over time, I have added to this list of assumptions, and I offer different ones based on the context in which I am sharing.

> ▶ We live in a toxic culture that affects us all. We are not encouraged to see it, so we must learn to see our culture and how it teaches us to transform the absurd into normal.
> ▶ We cannot bypass our suffering.
> ▶ The path of yoga is not time-limited. The path is ongoing and consistently asks the practitioner to deepen not only their awareness and consciousness but also their study of the practice.
> ▶ Spiritual practice reconnects us with our true nature.
> ▶ We are interconnected and interdependent.
> ▶ None of this is easy, and we have to do it anyway. In my experience, spiritual practice isn't easy because it asks me to do the work to understand the obstacles in the way of my and our liberation and to work to remove them. This means I must work to understand the suffering that creates obstacles to our liberation. Looking into the face of suffering isn't easy, but it is necessary for us to do if we want to be free.

Part One

The Root of Our Suffering
and the Five Kleshas

Part One offers an overview of the five kleshas, or obstacles, that create suffering for us individually and collectively. The overview also includes an outline of the eight-limbed path of yoga as an introduction to what we can begin to practice to decrease our suffering. After the overview, this section explores the first klesha—*avidya*, or ignorance. It invites the reader to deepen their understanding of how the root of our suffering is a lack of clear sight that leads to us believing we are separate from one another, from human and nonhuman beings, and from all that has been, is now, and will be. This section ends with several practices intended to develop your ability to see clearly and to remember how intricately interconnected everything and everyone truly is.

1

The Five Kleshas

We need suffering in order to see the path. The origin of suffering, the cessation of suffering, and the path leading to the cessation of suffering are all found in the heart of suffering. If we are afraid to touch our suffering, we will not be able to realize the path of peace, joy, and liberation. Don't run away. . . . Make peace with it.

—THICH NHAT HANH, *THE HEART OF THE BUDDHA'S TEACHING: TRANSFORMING SUFFERING INTO PEACE, JOY, AND LIBERATION*

AS THICH NHAT HANH so wisely taught, the pathway to the cessation of suffering and the end of suffering is actually found in the heart of the suffering. We are all suffering. We must accept that suffering is part of the human condition. Suffering is part of what we will encounter and experience in our human bodies at this time on the planet. We cannot bypass our suffering and expect to find freedom and peace. We will come to a place of understanding how to stop suffering when we begin to understand why we suffer so deeply and what causes our suffering.

This chapter invites us to begin to understand the five causes of suffering, known as the afflictions, or kleshas. This chapter explores how our suffering causes us great sorrow individually and collectively. We will begin with an explanation of each klesha in detail, followed by how the five kleshas lead to samskaras (tendencies) and the karma (the consequences) we experience due to our tendencies.

Five Reasons Why We Suffer

Avidya: *Ignorance*

Asmita: *An overidentification with ego*

Raga: *An attachment to desire or pleasure*

Dvesha: *Aversion or avoidance*

Abhinivesha: *A fear of letting go or a fear of death*

*Ignorance, egoism, attachment, hatred, and clinging
to bodily life are the five obstacles.*

—YOGA SUTRA 2.3, TRANSLATED BY SRI SWAMI SATCHIDANANDA
 IN *THE YOGA SUTRAS OF PATANJALI*

Avidya, or ignorance, derives from the belief that we are separate from one another and all that has been, is now, and will be. This belief is counter to what the practice of yoga invites us to do—see the ways we are connected to everyone and everything and come into union with all beings and their inherent divinity. In chapter 2, I will explain in great detail how avidya causes suffering and is an obstacle to our liberation.

Asmita is egoism. It is an overattachment to ego, which can look like an attachment to identifying with our work, the relationships we are in, or our roles. Sometimes it is defined as "I-amness." An overattachment to ego moves us away from our true nature, which is connected to everyone and everything. Asmita can lead us to become wedded to our individual experiences at the expense of our interconnectedness with all beings. In chapter 4, I will discuss asmita and the specific ways it shows up individually and collectively.

Raga is an attachment to desire or pleasure. Raga is rooted in us becoming attached to pleasure because we believe pleasurable things (which are fleeting) will bring us happiness. Furthermore, raga can cause us to expect pleasure to come only from outside forces, which doesn't allow us to find happiness within. In chapter 7, I will share more about how raga limits our ability to find samadhi, or liberation.

While raga is an attachment to pleasure, *dvesha* is defined as aversion or avoidance. Dvesha and raga are intertwined because our addiction to pleasure can lead to an aversion to the things we perceive as not bringing us pleasure. One might associate things they perceive as not bringing happiness to them as things to be avoided. Dvesha causes great suffering because we can become imbued with hate for what doesn't appear to bring us happiness. In chapter 10, I will explore how dvesha affects us individually and collectively and creates conditions for systems of dominance and superiority to thrive.

The final klesha is *abhinivesha*. This is translated as a fear of letting go or a fear of death. In my experience, I have been conditioned by the dominant Western culture to cling to things and resist the temporary nature of what I will experience in life. I have been conditioned to resist the idea that I will die one day, that this is an inevitable outcome—birth and death are part of the cycle of life. This resistance to death and even aversion to talking about the natural cycle of things, which includes physical death but also the death of relationships, jobs, and roles we play as well as transitions we might make in our lives, has become embedded in institutions and is infused in our norms around death and how we talk about letting go and loss. In chapter 13, I will share more about our fear of death and letting go and how this causes us to suffer.

The individual kleshas and ways we suffer do not occur in isolation. Avidya is shared first, and all of the other kleshas derive from avidya, the idea that we are separate from one another. We attach to the ego, asmita, and allow mental, physical, and emotional aspects of ourselves to be mistaken as our true nature. The misperception of who we are leads to raga, which impedes our ability to find happiness and peace within ourselves. We also express the misperception of who we are by becoming attached to pleasure, especially from outside sources, dvesha. This addiction doesn't allow us to remember that our natural state is one of peace and happiness. When we experience pleasure as temporary, we tend to dislike the people, situations, or experiences that we perceive as bringing unpleasantness into our lives. We learn to hate the things we think are in the way of us experiencing pleasure. We form aversions to that which we perceive inhibits us from feeling pleasure, even though pleasure is temporary. In our natural state, we can find steadiness and contentment even when we experience things that we perceive as unpleasant.

Our struggle with the temporary nature of things, experienced as raga and dvesha, causes us to develop unhealthy attachment patterns. Raga and dvesha also relate to the suffering we experience because of our resistance to change and the fact that everything we will experience in our physical bodies, emotionally, and mentally is temporary. Our resistance to change and our struggle with the temporary nature of things, which leads to difficulty in letting go, is abhinivesha.

Samskaras

The kleshas create patterns of behavior and tendencies called samskaras. As Pandit Rajmani Tigunait, the spiritual head of the Himalayan Institute and successor of Swami Rama of the Himalayas, explains, "Samskaras are the subtle impressions of our past actions. As long as we are alive, we continuously perform actions, but not all of them contribute to the formation of samskaras. Actions that we perform with full awareness are the ones that make the greatest impression on our minds. In other words, it is the intention behind the action that gives power to that action."[2] When we perform certain actions, it is believed that an impression is placed in our mindfield. Each time we repeat that same action, the impression in our mindfield becomes stronger. We form habits from these strong impressions. These actions can be cognitive, such as ways of thinking or repetitive thought patterns that lead to repetitive behaviors. For example, if I believe I will not succeed, and this is a thought that has made an impression in my mind, each time I try something new, the act of thinking that I will not succeed might get in the way of me trying something new. This thought about success, or rather, the assumption that I will be unsuccessful, drives my behavior and the actions I take in my life.

During COVID-19 I began to watch TV at night more frequently and consistently than before the pandemic. I would sit on the couch and watch TV as a way to pass the time instead of reading a book, chanting and playing harmonium, journaling, or even, at times, going to bed early. Often wine would accompany my TV watching, and then late-night snacks became part of this ritual. When this habit began, I didn't know we would continue to experience a pandemic and that many of us would be in isolation for so long. Before I knew it, two years had passed, and the habit of watching TV, drinking wine, and eating snacks well after dinnertime continued. I continued repeating the same action, which created a habit and tendency.

> Obstacles (kleshas) are the breeding ground for
> tendencies (samskaras) that give rise to actions and
> the consequences (karma) thereof. Such obstacles are
> experienced as visible or invisible obstacles.
> —YOGA SUTRA 2.12, OLIVIA HSU, "LEARN HOW THE KLESHAS CAN
> BOOST SELF-AWARENESS," YOGA JOURNAL, JANUARY 2, 2018.

The result of karma that derived from the samskara described above was a feeling of being spiritually empty instead of spiritually full and nourished. The wine and snacks didn't move me closer to my nature or God; in fact, mindlessly eating snacks and drinking wine made me feel tired and less likely to exercise or take good care of my body the next day. Sometimes we might crave nourishment from things like wine, TV, and snacks, which feels natural and very human. You may feel spiritually nourished by TV, wine, and snacks. After some time, I realized I wasn't spiritually nourished by these activities. As I reflect on it now, I believe this samskara resulted from avidya and raga. I actually had an experience of physical separation from people due to the need to socially isolate myself, and I believed the TV watching, wine, and snacks brought me pleasure. At times it is likely they did, but it was always temporary and led me to engage in this samskara without much thought because it had become a habit.

If you are someone who tried your best to cope with the pandemic and engaged in similar habits, I am not in a place of judgment about you, or really even myself. My nervous system was overwhelmed, and I was trying to cope with an experience that I didn't know how to fully integrate. While I am not in a place of judgment, I offer this as an example of how a repeated action can become habit and lead to karma that doesn't benefit one's spirit or connect one more deeply with their true nature.

Although samskaras aren't inherently negative, the pattern of behavior I described as a samskara is, for me, an example of a negative samskara. At times, that samskara led me to engage in patterns of behavior that contributed to more suffering on our planet. For example, during some of my late-night TV-watching escapades, I would also look on my phone and order various things from Amazon Prime. I wasn't even paying attention to the TV show and instead was looking at my phone while the TV played in the background. I could offer a ton of commentary about Amazon and Jeff Bezos, but instead of going to that place, I'll offer this: each time I senselessly clicked the "order" button on Amazon, I was less connected to the source of where I was ordering from, both the platform and the objects' actual origin, and whether I needed whatever I was ordering or not. I was thinking about convenience or, at times, just feeling like I wanted a distraction. I wasn't thinking about the local store I may have been able to support and purchase the item from. I wasn't thinking about the working conditions for the employees at Amazon. I wasn't thinking about the capitalistic system in which we live and how my click of a button was feeding a system that isn't focused on liberation or freedom. I am not suggesting that I am a callous person who wants to feed a capitalist machine. I am suggesting I am part of a capitalist system that I know is causing harm globally. I have participated in this system in senseless ways and ways that don't align with my values or the commitment I have made to practice the path of yoga and create conditions for justice.

If I have just described a samskara you engage in—ordering things without questioning where they come from and participating in the capitalist system—please know that I am not in a place of judgment; I am in a place of discernment and curiosity about how to create habits that support the collective good. As a collective, we engage in and are witness to samskaras that move us further away from our interconnectedness and are expressed through imbalances of social and institutional power, violence, warfare, capitalism, patterns of dominance, and systems of oppression. The path of yoga invites us to challenge our individual and collective samskaras so we can experience the consequences of actions (karma) that serve the collective good. Through the practice of yoga, we can create tendencies that form habits and impressions in our mindfield that support our and the collective's highest good. We will explore how to create new samskaras and decrease the impact of each klesha as well as how to shift the consequences of our actions (karma) in service of something bigger than ourselves throughout this book.

Karma

The womb of karmas (actions and reactions) has its root in
these obstacles, and the karmas bring experiences in the seen
[present] or in the unseen [future] births.
—YOGA SUTRA 2.12, TRANSLATED BY SRI SWAMI SATCHIDANANDA
IN *THE YOGA SUTRAS OF PATANJALI*

In the Yoga Sutras, karma is described as an action or the result of an action. These actions accumulate over time. We carry karma with us from one lifetime into the next until we are able to become unbound from the kleshas. This is when we reach the state of samadhi. Meesha Sharma, a Desi person and the creator of Alchemystic Studio, describes karma and what we can access when we break the cycle of suffering through the practice of the path of yoga: "Karma is a cycle in which one is reborn over and over on Earth until they can break the cycle and return to the divine source from which we are all birthed."[3] Breaking this cycle requires us to learn to mitigate our individual and collective suffering, remember our true nature, and reset our karmic path so we can return to our divinity and the divine source from which we are all birthed.

Yoga philosophy teaches us that if we do not work to remove obstacles or mitigate the kleshas, we will carry our suffering from this lifetime onto the next—not just for ourselves but for the collective and future generations. We may not always be aware of the karma we are working through from previous lifetimes in our present lifetime; the path of yoga teaches us to create samskaras that cultivate positive karma and result in all beings and the earth being in a liberated state. We can create these samskaras and karmic results if we commit ourselves to the eight-limbed path of yoga. This path can "nullify the effects of our negative karma."[4]

The Eight-Limbed Path of Yoga

By the practice of the limbs of Yoga, the impurities dwindle away and there
dawns the light of wisdom, leading to discriminative discernment.
—YOGA SUTRA 2.28, TRANSLATED BY SRI SWAMI SATCHIDANANDA
IN *THE YOGA SUTRAS OF PATANJALI*

This sutra provides the antidote to our afflictions. Patanjali taught that the kleshas are obstacles and hindrances. The eight-limbed path of yoga provides the tools and practices we need to work to overcome these hindrances, thus allowing us to gain more wisdom about our true nature, divinity, and inherent interconnectedness to all beings. This is what I believe creates an opportunity for us to work toward creating conditions for our collective freedom, samadhi.

As shared in the introduction, I offer my understanding of the kleshas, Yoga Sutras, and path of yoga from my specific worldview. I consistently strive to contextualize the teachings of the path of yoga so they can be applied to the context in which we currently live. I do not posit to know everyone's lived experience of the specific context in which they exist. Below, I will share my interpretation of the eight-limbed path of yoga as I understand it. My interpretation is based on my belief that samadhi is connected to liberation, not solely mine but ours. My interpretation of the path is informed by my experience of injustice in an unjust world and the ways I have both caused and been on the receiving end of suffering. You may have a different understanding of the path of yoga because of your experience with the practice, the lineage of yoga you practice, and the knowledge you have gained from the practice.

The eight-limbed path includes:

1. **The Yamas:** The *Yamas* focus on our interactions with others. They are observances focused on how we treat others and the world around us. In many ways, they speak to how we can create a world with less suffering by realizing how our actions affect others and the world around us.

   Ahimsa: Non-violence, non-harming through actions, thoughts, and words. Ahimsa is the absence of injustice, violence, and cruelty. This includes actions, words, and ways of living. Ahimsa means always behaving in a way that takes into account whether your behavior is causing harm or injustice. Ahimsa asks us to consider how harm is already a part of the cultural context, who is experiencing the most harm and why, and what our responsibility is in creating less harm for people and our planet. Ahimsa isn't solely focused on the individual; it applies to decreasing the ways different groups of people are harmed due to how structures and systems of dominance have been set up to oppress those less proximal to power and benefit those in closer proximity to power. Ahimsa is intended to free us all of harm.

Satya: Truthfulness; satya means "to speak the truth." Dominant culture perpetuates the belief that there is one narrative. Often this serves to silence those who are less proximal to power. Moving beyond the idea that only one truth exists allows us to create a space for dialogue, authenticity, learning, opening, and understanding. Acknowledging the truth of how we came to be in a space with so much suffering, the ways we perpetuate suffering, and how suffering is experienced by different groups of people and the planet is a practice of satya. We will be unable to free ourselves from suffering if we are unwilling to speak the truth about why it occurs and what keeps it in place.

Asteya: Non-stealing, not taking more than you need or more than is freely offered. Asteya is about not stealing or taking anything that doesn't belong to us, but its focus goes beyond material possessions. Asteya looks at all levels of our being. It applies to the earth and the ways we are in an extractive relationship with the earth. It applies to a history of taking land and resources due to systems like white supremacy and capitalism and the lack of reparations to those who have been most harmed by these systems. Asteya challenges us to be mindful of our choices around what we consume, take, need, and desire, and to contemplate how what we take, need, or consume affects the collective.

Brahmacharya: Energy management; managing extremes, cravings, specifically sexual energy. The practice of brahmacharya calls us to honor the sanctity of our life force by managing our energy. Brahmacharya is composed of two parts: the first is the root *car*, which means "to move," and the second is *brahma*, which means "truth." Brahmacharya is the movement toward essential truth— the truth that we are divine beings and our journey is meant to be one in which we move with God's consciousness. To walk in God's consciousness, we must withdraw our senses, manage our energy, and try to find balance through something other than giving in to our cravings.

Aparigraha: Non-possessiveness, non-grasping, letting go of attachment. Aparigraha builds on the intent of asteya. It encourages one to assess unhealthy attachments, negative thinking or old belief patterns, fears, and desires. Dominant culture thrives because of a belief in scarcity. Aparigraha invites one to believe in abundance. I am not suggesting magical thinking in the sense of, if we want an abundant life, we can have one. It isn't as simple as that. Structures such as capitalism are in place to keep those who are not experiencing abundance in a place of not having enough. Aparigraha invites us to consider how we might redistribute resources such that everyone has what they need.

2. **The *Niyamas*:** The Niyamas are observances focused on how we treat ourselves.

Saucha: Purification; cleanliness in body, mind, and emotions. Saucha means "cleanliness." Saucha refers to a practice of cleanliness so we can more clearly access the divine source and see the divinity within others. The yoga asanas and pranayama are essential means through which we can attend to inner and outer saucha.

Santosha: Contentment. Santosha is the practice of acceptance. It is being able to be with things as they are. I am not suggesting we do not need to also make changes for the greater good, but what often causes suffering is a lack of contentment with the way things are, what we possess, how we look, and what is happening in our lives. I believe when one is clear about the truth of the moment, they can ask themselves what necessary changes for the greater good are within their power to make.

Tapas: Will, passion, perseverance, heat in the practice. Tapas is one of the most powerful concepts in the Yoga Sutras. The word *tapas* comes from the Sanskrit verb *tap*, which means "to burn." The traditional interpretation of *tapas* is "fiery discipline." Tapas relates to the process by which we burn away impurities, thus decreasing our suffering and creating a pathway toward samadhi.

Svadhyaya: Self-study, absorbing spiritual wisdom, nonjudgmental self-observation. Svadhyaya is the practice of self-reflection. It is the study of the Self. The practice of studying oneself allows one to witness and see the obstacles and patterns of suffering that are in the way of one experiencing samadhi. I would extend this understanding and offer that the study of oneself in relationship to the collective allows one to see and dismantle what is in the way of collective samadhi. Svadhyaya invokes a process of attainment of wisdom by expanding and not being controlled by the mind and our social conditioning and shaping. This practice allows one to see themselves more clearly and to connect with the divine within, which will allow them to see the divine spark that exists in all beings.

Ishvara Pranidhana: Surrender to God or Spirit, offering up the fruits of your actions to something greater. Ishvara Pranidhana means to surrender to a higher source, to "lay all of your actions at the feet of God/the Divine." In moving closer to the Divine, one is able to work toward a higher purpose focused on our shared humanity and the oneness of all beings.

3. **Asana:** The physical postures. Patanjali taught that the postures should be practiced with a balance of ease, *sukha*, and effort, *stira*.

4. **Pranayama:** Breath control. *Prana* is translated as "life force" or "energy." We feel this in our bodies each time we are able to consciously and deeply breathe. When we are unable to breathe fully and deeply, our life force is limited or restricted. Pranayama practices are meant to support us in mindfully breathing to calm the nervous system and still the mind. In addition, I believe we can work with the breath to better understand how another's life force is being limited based on their proximity to power and social location. We live during a time when social movements, such as Black Lives Matter, call for Black people to have the space to breathe.

This is due to the fact that dominant culture deems many people to be inferior; as such, Black people and many other groups have been robbed of the breath. While an individual pranayama practice might be focused on mindful breathing for oneself, I encourage you to consider how breathing more deeply aids and supports creating conditions for others to have space to breathe freely. The capacity to breathe freely equates with the capacity to move and be free.

5. *Pratyahara*: Inward focus. Pratyahara is the withdrawal of the senses so we can turn inward and move away from the noise of the world. The world is overwhelming at times, and if we are not in a place of steadiness, we can become swept up in the overwhelm and be driven by our senses instead of by our divine nature. The practice of pratyahara invites us to turn inward in our effort to develop more compassion and a sense of steadiness instead of reactivity. The practice of pratyahara creates an opportunity for us to be responsive to the outer world instead of being swept up in our reaction to the ever-changing nature of the world and our human experience of it. Pratyahara is different from bypassing the reality in which we live. It is instead a process whereby we can turn inward, develop the skill of equanimity and evenness of mind and body, and respond to the spiritual crisis we face with skillfulness and care.

6. *Dharana*: Concentration. Dharana is described as deep concentration or a single-pointed focus of the mind. Dharana isn't about turning off the mind; it is instead about deciding where we want to focus our attention. Meditation begins with deep concentration, and it empowers one to see things and think clearly. This practice works to free us from ignorance and misperceptions.

7. *Dhyana*: Deeper concentration, or meditation. Dhyana is the act of sustained focus on a single point. This occurs through the practice of meditation. At times, the practice of meditation enables one to transcend the physical body and trappings of the mind. Dhyana is the practice of finding peace and steadiness through meditation. The ability to free oneself from the mind and body could create

space for us to dream beyond the current cultural and political context and the conditions in place that prevent us from finding or creating collective freedom. In some ways, I believe we must dream outside of the confines of ourselves and the toxicity we have inherited to create a world in which we all can be free. My own practice of meditation is meant to open up a space for this kind of dreaming and to contemplate what is possible beyond what I can see or am experiencing at any given moment. In this way, we transcend cultural conditioning that keeps us in a place of suffering and work to create a culture that centers collective care and the ways we are inextricably bound to one another.

8. **Samadhi:** Bliss or liberation. Often samadhi is translated as a state of oneness or bliss. I like to think of samadhi as liberation, because wouldn't it be blissful for us all to feel free? Not at the expense of one another but because we recognize the inherent connection between ourselves and all beings. I have a very vivid memory of experiencing samadhi, a time when I could feel my connection with everything and everyone. I was in a meditation led by a friend. She was playing a musical instrument. I heard the birds outside accompanying the music my friend was playing. I felt the sunshine streaming in through the window. I felt relaxed and at peace; for a moment, I felt as if I was the birds, sunshine, and musical notes. I felt in union with everything around me, and it felt beautiful. This is what I long for—for us to feel our connection and union with everything around us. We live in a world full of division that causes us a grave amount of suffering. The eight-limbed path and a consistent practice of yoga will support us in experiencing moments, if not hours and days, of samadhi. I don't expect us to be in a sustained state of samadhi. I am not sure even the greatest yoga practitioners and teachers have ever achieved samadhi. I am suggesting what Patanjali taught: that we can strive to remember our oneness and come back into union with all that surrounds us. We can see ourselves in each other. We can feel our sacred divinity as an extension of the divinity contained within everything.

Kriya Yoga

Yoga in action is composed of austerity, self-study and trustful surrender to Ishvara.

—YOGA SUTRA 2.1, TRANSLATED BY PANDIT RAJMANI TIGUNAIT, *THE PRACTICE OF THE YOGA SUTRA: SADHANA PADA*

The eight-limbed path in its entirety is what we need to practice to achieve samadhi. Even so, I would be remiss if I didn't mention here that in Book Two of the Yoga Sutras, Patanjali highlights three parts of the path describing Kriya Yoga. These parts are tapas, svadhyaya, and Ishvara Pranidhana. Pandit Rajmani Tigunait describes Kriya as "the ability to act and the ability to move. Kriya Yoga is an action plan for acquiring a calm and tranquil mind; an action plan for reaching an absolutely still state of mind."[5]

Patanjali's Yoga Sutras teach us to acquire a calm and tranquil mind through tapas—purification, transformation, and the discipline to continue to change our minds and bodies through the ever-changing experience of being human. Patanjali taught that one must practice svadhyaya to study themselves and deepen their understanding of their internal landscape and their relationship with and experience of the outer world. The final component of Kriya Yoga mentioned in verse 2.1 is Ishvara Pranidhana. In the context of Kriya Yoga and the eight-limbed path, it is surrender to Spirit or God. This does not mean we can be passive about what is happening internally and in the outer world of which we are a part. *Ishvara* is devotion to God or something bigger than oneself. It is the belief that a divine force is working to guide and protect us, but we must do our part. We must consistently devote our actions to Spirit or God, that which is bigger than us. It is my understanding that Patanjali placed a focus on tapas, svadhyaya, and Ishvara Pranidhana because they are core components of yoga, and Patanjali also outlined the path of Ashtanga, the eight-limbed path of yoga, which includes Kriya Yoga.

REFLECTION QUESTIONS

The subsequent chapters will explore each klesha and offer practices from this path to support you as you work toward a world with less suffering. For now, I invite you to consider and assess where you are on your path of the study of yoga. This is not a test. It is the practice of svadhyaya. It is intended to provide a pause for you to reflect on how the eight-limbed path has assisted and is assisting you in understanding the ways you suffer and contribute to our collective suffering, and the ways you might begin to mitigate the experience of suffering for yourself and others.

Take some time to respond to the following reflection questions:

▶ What parts of the eight-limbed path am I currently practicing consistently?

▶ In what ways is my practice working to address my suffering and the suffering of others?

▶ How might I enhance my current practice of yoga?

2

Avidya

Woven into our lives is the very fire from the stars and genes
from the sea creatures, and everyone, utterly everyone,
is kin in the radiant tapestry of being
—ELIZABETH JOHNSON, *WOMAN, EARTH, AND CREATOR SPIRIT*

I RECENTLY VISITED THE island of Kauai with a few of my closest
friends. I've actually spent a lot of time on this island, but up until
this most recent trip, it had been thirty-three years since I had last
visited. I knew that, going there, I would feel some complicated emotions and feelings, and while I longed for the land because it was one
of my childhood homes, I knew the land wasn't mine. The legacy of
colonialism in Hawaii is inescapable. The word "plantation" appears on
street signs, at the entrance of gated communities, and in pamphlets
about various sites to visit while one is on the island. There is a righteous anger and resentment permeating throughout the air, clearly
related to the constant influx of tourists. There is a tension present in
Hawaii that feels viscous, almost like tar. This tension is juxtaposed with
an earthly paradise where breathtaking beauty and open-hearted locals
exist everywhere.

I went to visit or revisit Kauai because it significantly influenced me as
a child. When I was young, I spent summers, holidays, and other times
there for many years in a row. I stopped visiting my father in Kauai in

1989, but he lived on the island until 1992, when Hurricane Iniki—meaning "strong and piercing wind"—hit the island and took off the second story of my father's house. After the storm, my father relocated to Prescott, Arizona. This time, when I visited Kauai after so many years, I felt like a foreigner on land that is not native to my blood lineage; at the same time, I felt a deep familiarity with the land and the people native to it. I visited in hopes of reconnecting with the land and reconnecting with my father's spirit and energy.

While in Kauai, my friends and I went to visit Wailua Falls. *Wailua* means "twin" or "two rivers." The waterfall is on the south end of the Wailua River. The land where the falls flow was one of the primary religious and political centers on the island. The remains of a sacred temple and of religious sites still exist along the Wailua River. We ventured out to see the breathtaking falls and traveled up a windy road to get to them. On this windy road, we saw signs that clearly indicated no hiking was allowed down to the falls. These signs also indicated that hiking could be dangerous or even life-threatening. When we arrived at the falls, we saw people walking past one of the no-hiking signs and behind a chain-linked fence to a muddy and steep incline. I perceived the signs as a warning to deter folks from hiking down the steep, muddy hill and as a boundary meant to protect the sacred land.

My friends and I had no interest in disrespecting the land or disregarding the posted signs, rules, or boundaries. I stood at the concrete wall and looked down to take in the waterfall and the white-tailed tropic birds floating like kites on currents of wind. While I took in the beautiful scenery and view of the land, two of my friends went over to investigate what was happening near one of the no-hiking signs along the fence. Ultimately, these friends ended up confronting some of the people who were clearly disregarding the signs and attempting to hike down to the waterfall. I say "attempt" because we saw some people who had begun the hike down and quickly come back up after realizing how dangerous it could be for them to go any further.

My friend, Alexis, asked a man who was venturing behind the fence if he had seen the no-hiking sign. At first, he didn't answer her, but she felt clear he had heard her. She went on to say, "It is disrespectful to disregard the sign. It is disrespectful to the land." He piped up because he had heard her first question and follow-up commentary about disrespecting the land, and he said, "I know it is."

My jaw dropped when she reported back to me about the interaction and the fact that the man she confronted had willingly acknowledged he was disrespecting the land. Though I don't know if I was surprised. At this point, the blatant disrespect people express toward the planet shouldn't surprise me because it happens so often. It happens so much that many of us have become desensitized to how our actions impact the planet. Although I wasn't surprised, I felt hurt for the sacred land and the waterfall that flows from it. I felt hurt for the birds floating through the air with the wind. I felt hurt for the tiny plants being stepped on by the footsteps of people who wanted to say they had hiked down to the falls. I felt hurt for the parts of the ecosystem that may be invisible to us but were present on that land. I felt hurt for the people indigenous to the land. I reflected on the labor the Indigenous people of Kauai have had to expend to rescue foreigners who disregard posted signs and don't honor the land's sanctity.

The man who consciously chose to disrespect the land, and all of the other people who aren't native to the land who make this same choice, likely do not feel as if the rules apply to them and don't feel a deep connection to the land. The land is something to traverse, even if it is dangerous or one might step on sacred plants or areas of restoration. The land is something on which one can step and use for their own pleasure. These people feel as if they are separate from the land and from nature and that they are entitled to treat the land as they wish. When we don't feel as if we are one with land and the energy of Spirit that runs through it, it is easier to disrespect the land. When we don't feel a connection to a people who are as divine as us, it is easier to disrespect the people. When we disrespect any living being, we are disrespecting ourselves. This disrespect emerges from the ways we have become disembodied from our spirits, Spirit, the higher consciousness, and the oneness in all things.

Ignorance

The story I've shared about Kauai isn't unique to Kauai or to other native lands. The ignorance and disrespect expressed by the tourist we encountered there isn't new human behavior but rather a pattern deriving from profound disconnection from not only the land, people, and the entire planet but also ourselves and the truth of who we are. As explained in the introduction, *avidya* translates to mean ignorance. This ignorance is based on the idea that we believe we are separate from one another. This is a misperception of the mind. Avidya, ignorance, is a distortion of the mind. We have misperceived who we are, and we are in a spiritual crisis because of this. Avidya prevents us from being able to see ourselves as part of a collective and the higher consciousness that lives inside all things, everywhere. Avidya represents us believing an illusion and not clearly seeing what is true. The illusion that we are separate from one another and not part of all things and connected with a higher consciousness leads us to operate from our lower ego: For example, I want to hike this land, and it doesn't matter if I disrespect it. Furthermore, I deserve to hike this, and even when someone challenges me about it and calls me back to remember my connection with the land, I will dismiss them because I am separate from them, too.

We have been conditioned to believe the illusion that we are separate. This conditioning has taken place from messages we receive about who we are—for example, we are individuals and not in relationship with one another, or what we do doesn't matter nor have an impact on others. We have been conditioned by cultural norms that value individualism over relationships and connections. Systems such as capitalism are profiting from the illusion that we are separate. We have been conditioned to uphold the hierarchies of people, species, and power.

The system of white supremacy and the hierarchy of race was predicated on the belief that white-bodied humans were more divine and pure than Black bodies, Indigenous bodies, and bodies of color. The construction of gender is a manifestation of patriarchy and the desire to control bodies through sexism and heterosexism. The hierarchy of human bodies over the earth came from a disconnection from our sacred relationship with the earth and a desire to mine the earth of its resources as if its resources aren't valuable and are only to be used for our enjoyment or capital gain. The hierarchy of religion coupled with colonization has led Christianity to be used as a tool of oppression, furthering the perception that we are separate from one another and that there is one faith and one God that is superior to all others. Those who do not believe in the Christian God have been persecuted and ridiculed throughout history.

The ways we have been conditioned and shaped have contributed to hierarchies that breed inequity and an imbalance of power. This is based on the belief that power should be held only by certain people and in certain places, and this further perpetuates the idea that we are separate. This flawed belief has led to how institutions and systems have been built worldwide. Institutions have internalized a belief in the hierarchy of bodies, leading them to stratify power and create structures where our very experience of reality is defined by how much power we have to control others through policies and practices we put in place within an institution or structure and how many resources we have and how we allocate them. This has resulted in economic peril for many, a housing crisis, the bailout by the federal government of banks and corporations, an ineffective social service system, further mining of the earth's resources, and inequity of all kinds.

Hierarchies have become embedded in cultural norms and ways of being—in who is seen as normal and human and who is not; in who is seen as valid and valuable and who is not. Cultural norms uphold the idea that some cultural practices and ways of being are superior to others. In addition, avidya has created cultural norms that make us erase the truth and history and instead rely on narratives that support further separation. For example, critical race theory has been in the news for several years now. It isn't a new theory. Bringing it up is a tactic of the alt-right agenda to erase the history of the race construct and to deny the true experience of Black, Indigenous, and communities of color because of a system like racism. This is just one example of how narratives have been changed and denied to uphold hierarchies and to maintain a state of ignorance.

Our Spiritual Crisis

Avidya is at the heart of the spiritual crisis we are experiencing now. The spiritual crisis we are facing and experiencing at this time derives from a crisis of consciousness about who we indeed are. Yoga philosophy and various other spiritual traditions teach us that we are the larger or Highest Self and that the Self represents our highest consciousness and oneness with all things. The lower ego, which we will explore more in chapter 4 when we dive in to asmita, is connected to believing I am my body, thoughts, mind, senses, desires, identities, and attachments. The Self represents the cosmic, spiritual, and universal consciousness of which we are all a part. Uniting the lower ego and the Higher Self through the path of yoga allows us to come into integrity and oneness. This unification of the lower ego and Higher Self is where we find freedom and spiritual enlightenment. The spiritual crisis of consciousness we face emerges from forgetting that we are a larger Self—something more than our bodies, thoughts, minds, senses, desires, identities, where we are in time and space, and our attachments. Avidya prevents us from remembering our true nature of *moksha*, liberation, and constrains our ability to create conditions for collective liberation.

It is painful to believe the misperception that I am separate, untethered, and disconnected from a source—the cosmic, universal, and spiritual consciousness. One might move through the world without ever feeling embodied physically and experience a lack of physical connection with the world around them. When we feel untethered and disconnected from our bodies, we are unable to see our connection with other living bodies and beings. What manifests from this disembodiment and separation on a large and systemic scale is humans enacting various forms of oppression and participating in and perpetuating systems of dominance. This behavior leads to an imbalance in our ecosystem, and we—especially those less proximal to social and institutional power—and the planet are experiencing grave consequences because of this. Bodies of land and water are physically impaired because we believe we aren't in deep connection with them. Species in our ecosystem are experiencing our abusive behavior, which has led some species to become extinct, and other species to try to adapt to untenable circumstances due to the irreparable ways we have changed the climate.

The pain one might experience because they believe they are separate from the world around them might lead them to feel emotions such as sadness, anger, resentment, disillusionment, and confusion, causing an emotional crisis. These emotions could lead to a mental crisis, such as depression, anxiety, or disassociation. Mental health crises happen for various reasons, and I will suggest that one of the reasons is because of avidya. The emotions mentioned above could lead to mental and cognitive distortions and lead one to suffer.

When we are not attuned to our connection with the cosmic, universal, and spiritual consciousness, we are less likely to be attuned to our own intuition or even understand we are intuitive beings who have inner wisdom that comes from a connection with the larger and Highest Self. Self is connected to every part of the Universe. When I forget that I am not my ego, desires, attachments, senses, or body, and forget there is another part of me—my Higher Self—I am not in union; instead, I am in a state of separation from myself, the Self, the inner truth of who I am, and the outer truth that we are connected to all things, always.

Yoga Sutra 2.5 explains avidya and further misperceptions that come from the belief we are separate from one another instead of a continuous stream of the eternal and universal consciousness.

> Ignorance is taking The Non-Eternal, The Impure,
> The Painful, The Non-Self, as The Eternal, The Pure,
> The Pleasurable and The Self.
> —YOGA SUTRA 2.5, TRANSLATED BY PARISAMVAD,
> THE YOGA INSTITUTE, THEYOGAINSTITUTE.ORG

This sutra speaks to what is planted and takes root when we operate from a place of separation and to the link between avidya and the other kleshas. The non-eternal is connected to the misperception that our souls are not everlasting and that our spirits aren't connected to a higher consciousness. Believing our souls are non-eternal makes us cling to life in a way that doesn't honor the natural cycle of life and death. Impurity relates to our inability to remember that all things are pure and divine, and to remember the shared divinity within all things. Pleasure and pain are connected to raga and dvesha and what occurs when we live from a place of separation, only wanting things that bring us pleasure and wanting to push away that which is painful and even developing an aversion to it.

This brings me back to the anecdote described at the beginning of this chapter—the operationalization of avidya, the belief that one is separate from sacred land such as the island of Kauai and the individual's desire to walk upon it in a way that is disrespectful. This desire overruled the individual's inner wisdom and the universal truth that they were part of that land, that they themselves are sacred not as an individual but as part of the higher consciousness and larger Self and source from which we all come. Avidya is at the heart of our suffering, and *vidya*—which describes what it is like to remember oneness—and the Higher Self are what will support us in remembering who we truly are. The presence of avidya begs the question of how we will heal, given how embedded separation and disconnection are in our individual and collective experience and way of being.

We will explore this in the next chapter. What feels important to remind you of now is that neither avidya nor any of the other kleshas are inherent to who we truly are. The kleshas and our samskaras are meant to be witnessed as we become the seer and investigator of our human experience and of whether or not the actions we take are in alignment with our Higher Self or in direct opposition to it. Through this process of awareness, we can begin to change both our inner and outer worlds and mitigate some of the suffering that is present here and now. We can shift our karmic path and move in a way that honors our divinity, humanity, and the divinity contained within everything.

> The aim of Yoga is to reach that state where our
> actions are not based on Avidya.
> —T. KRISHNAMACHARYA, "YOGA FREENOTES," YOGASTUDIES.ORG

REFLECTION QUESTIONS

Spiritual practice is a tool that allows us to better understand our human experience while living into the truth that we are part of a higher consciousness that is webbed together and includes all that has been, is, and will be. In chapter 3, we will explore how to engage the practice to remember our union with all things. For now, I invite you to reflect on the following questions. Consider how you have been shaped to believe you are separate, and contemplate how the way you have been shaped affects the way you move and navigate your inner and outer world.

▶ How have you been shaped to believe you are separate from other individuals and the planet?

▶ How has your shaping influenced your belief or connection to the truth that we are in a deep relationship with all things, past, present, and future?

▶ What has your experience in institutions been, and how have institutions influenced a belief that you are separate?

▶ What have cultural norms taught you about your relationship with others and the world around you?

▶ What has been lost (individually and collectively) due to how you have been conditioned by dominant culture and the belief that we are separate from one another and all things?

▶ What grief do you notice as you connect to the ways you have been shaped to believe you are separate instead of in union with all things?

▶ What might be possible as you remember you are in union with all things?

3

Vidya

The universe is wholly interconnected.

—LAURENCE GALIAN, *BEYOND DUALITY:*
THE ART OF TRANSCENDENCE

DURING PARTICULARLY DIFFICULT times in my life, when I've felt what seemed to be irreparable heartbreak, I've sought out the healing balm that only the expanse of the natural world can offer. In 2013, when the world felt utterly upside down and my nervous system was constantly overstimulated by the news cycle, unrelenting acts of violence against Black bodies, and the immense suffering on the planet, I sought out a mountain to heal my heart. Pilot Mountain was the mountain I visited whenever I could. I didn't know why at the time. I later learned that Pilot Mountain, which I frequented from 2013 to 2016, was a remnant of the Sauratown Mountains. The Saura people knew the mountain as Jomeokee, meaning Great Guide or Pilot. It indeed guided me out of dark spaces that felt inescapable. It guided me back home to myself time and time again.

In 2014, I hit my head and subsequently suffered a concussion. I was trying to heal my brain while managing my overwhelm in response to what felt like a very noisy world. The overwhelm led me to seek out the quiet of the country. While there, I received what I know as spiritual and healing medicine from the horses who lived on the land, the warmth of a wood-fired sauna fed by wood from the land, and snowy walks through the woods. The land's energy didn't match that of the clamorous world.

It was quiet and still in a way the world wasn't. It provided the precise quietness and stillness I needed, along with profound beauty—beauty held within the tall field grasses and the huge tree atop a hill that I would sit under to watch the sunlight dance through the trees as the sun rose each morning and set each evening.

In 2016, while navigating a massive transition in my marriage at the time, I moved out of the only house I had known for the previous sixteen years and into an apartment. During this transitional period, I sought out the creek bed, river rocks, deer, woodpeckers, and the sound of the breeze rustling through the trees. I sat on a bench at Bolin Creek in Carrboro, North Carolina, which brought me back to myself each instance I visited it. I shared musings, secrets, sorrows, and synchronicities with the woods and nature spirits.

In 2017, when I moved to Portland, Oregon, I received healing medicine from Mt. Hood, which I could see in the distance when I would walk through the forest near my house. Mt. Hood and other Pacific Northwest mountains had a way of working with my immense heartbreak and suffering that, at that time, felt unfamiliar to me. Similar to Pilot Mountain, the mountains in the Pacific Northwest served as a guide, but they felt much harsher in their approach. The mountain range was difficult for me to traverse. I hadn't ever experienced weather quite like the snowy conditions on Mt. Hood. The Pacific Northwest mountains emitted sorrow and grief to me, which mirrored the profound process I was moving through as I responded to unexpected loss and the subsequent grief and sorrow that followed. While living in Oregon, in addition to the medicine from the snowy and massive Pacific Northwest mountains, I also received medicine from the most enormous snails I have ever seen, the mist on the forest leaves, and the smell of firs, yews, and pines.

These are just a few examples of when the natural world has strived to bring me back to my own true nature. When the world makes no sense to me, all I have to do is look out the window, stand in my yard, listen to birdsong, watch a squirrel scurry up a utility pole or tree with a hickory nut, hear the sound of an acorn hitting the ground, breathe in the sweet smell of honey near my beehives, climb a hill or mountain, or visit a stream to remember the natural order of things and my place here on this planet. Nature has brought me back to my own divine connection with God, and it doesn't have to work hard to remind me of my relationship with everyone and everything.

As we explored in chapter 2, avidya is ignorance that derives from the belief we are separate. Nature reminds us there is no such thing as separation and that we are all part of a vast ecosystem. The natural world has the power to call us back into a deep connection with our inner wisdom and the wisdom present in the outer world. *Vidya*, the opposite of avidya, translates to "clarity" or "right knowledge." Vidya is about clear sight. The ability to see clearly allows us not only to see what is true and right but also the things that cloud our perception. Vidya is the awareness of the absolute truths that exist, like the fact that we are pure consciousness and that a Higher Self connected to our souls exists. Truths like we are nature, and there is no separation between us and all the elements of the natural world named earlier in this chapter. I am not separate from you or anything that has ever been or will be. We are part of an endless continuum of cosmic consciousness and creation. Vidya is not simply about intellectually understanding the truths mentioned above; vidya is an entire body and spirit awareness, an understanding of these truths. It is the difference between knowing something on a surface level and fully knowing something in our bones and beyond such that it changes who and how we are as beings.

In Book Two of the Yoga Sutras, Patanjali not only shares the origin of our afflictions and what is in the way of us experiencing freedom, he also shares about two forces that exist and have led to the creation of all things, *purusha* and *prakriti*. *Purusha* is translated as the true Self, supreme or soul consciousness. It is all that exists beyond the body and mind. It contains consciousness that is void of ego. Pure consciousness. *Prakriti* is translated as nature or matter comprised of different qualities, the *gunas*. These different qualities of matter, the gunas, are *sattva* (pure, light energy), *rajas* (heat, agitation), *and tamas* (dullness).

> Pain that has not yet come is avoidable.
>
> The cause of that avoidable pain is the union of the Seer (Purusha) and the Seen (Prakriti or Nature).
>
> —YOGA SUTRA 2.16 AND 2.17, TRANSLATED BY SRI SWAMI SATCHIDANANDA IN *THE YOGA SUTRAS OF PATANJALI*

Prakriti can be thought of as the mind and body in relationship to purusha, our higher or soul's consciousness, connected to pure and supreme consciousness, or God. Purusha is the divine spark that creates all things, and prakriti is what is manifested and created. As beings housed in human bodies, at times we mistake our experience of being human in physical form, and the mind perceives itself as if it is the whole of our experience and our true nature. We confuse our minds and bodies with what is pure and supreme consciousness. The practice of yoga teaches us to become the witness to our human experience so we can remember our soul's consciousness as something more vast than our physical bodies, so we can remember the essence of our true nature and the true nature of all things, which is *sattva*, pure love and light.

I encounter many practitioners of yoga who have an intellectual understanding that our true nature is one of love and light and that our natural state is one of peace and harmony. At a minimum, many have an intellectual understanding of pure consciousness and the divine spark in all things, because this is what the path of yoga has taught them. Many of us who identify as students or teachers of yoga understand that one intention of the practice is to support us in operating from a place of pure and higher consciousness so that we may suffer less individually and collectively. It is essential to understand that our true nature *is* one of pure consciousness and divinity, and that this is the true nature of all beings, but vidya is also about how we use our knowledge and ability to see clearly.

When we experience vidya—an alignment with right knowledge derived from an awareness of ourselves and all beings as spiritual and divine and part of pure consciousness—this knowledge can and should direct the actions we take in our lives and the world. A practice focused on becoming more clear about our inner wisdom and the higher, irrefutable truths of our interconnectedness with God and pure consciousness lifts the veil, avidya, the illusion we are separate. Vidya, clear sight, removes the illusion that we are not nature. Clear sight leads us to understand that the ways we cause suffering are not true to our nature. "Vidya cancels the veiling quality of avidya; thus the experience it brings leads to liberation. The light of vidya, intuitive wisdom, shines forth in proportion to the attenuation of avidya, the fundamental force of affliction. In other words, the veiling effects of avidya are attenuated in direct proportion to the radiant light of intuitive wisdom."[6]

I sought out the natural world during times of great suffering as a practice to bring me back home to the truth of who I am. The natural world returned me to my higher consciousness and Self. The natural world reminded me of my own radiant light, my own divine spark, and the collective wisdom derived from the pure consciousness contained in all I encountered as I traversed various landscapes, sat next to myriad rivers and streams, and perused the sky for winged ones. The suffering we experience because of all that is in the way (self-imposed or put upon us by systems, conditioning, and generational patterns) of us tapping into our inner wisdom, pure consciousness, and deep knowledge does not have to be our pathway or destiny. Suffering is something we experience because we confuse prakriti with purusha. In other words, we confuse our physical experience in bodies and our cognitions or mind-matter with pure consciousness. Vidya brings us into a space of remembering true consciousness and the pure consciousness found in all things.

The natural world would mirror back pure consciousness to me through its resilience, adaptability, grace, ferocity, connection, and interdependence. It reflected my own embodied pure consciousness through how Spirit coursed through me and every part of the ecosystem. Nature reminds me I am not just an individual in physical form. It reminds me of the ways I am in deep relationship with it. It reminds me that I inhabit all of the elements of the natural world inside my physical form. I am steady and strong, just like the mountains I would climb and sit atop. I am the clearing, the vista at the top of the mountain. We are the expanse of mountain ranges and as deep as valleys. I am water. I was born of water, protected by the fluid in my mother's womb. We are water. I am the wind rustling through the trees. My inhales and exhales allow air to pass through me and us. We are the wind. I am the many stones I have found on the earth while walking upon it. I ponder the bigger rock formation from which these stones came and am reminded of my own lineage and that I am part of something much bigger. We are part of something bigger.

When the world would narrow and my heart was suffering, the mountains would expand my consciousness and operate not only as a healing salve but as a doorway to higher consciousness, seeded with tools to live into my commitment to decreasing suffering for myself and others. When I felt isolated, a butterfly or buzzing bee would flit by me to let me know that I am never alone and am always in connection with all things. I am the butterfly and the buzzing bee. When I sat in a place of ignorance, giving in to the lie that we are separate, a hawk would fly overhead as if to say, "Broaden your perspective; you can see more from up here, up higher, closer to God and Spirit." The hawk would remind me of my connection with it, and that I was indeed the hawk just as I was the mountain, the ocean, fire, ether, earth, trees, and the above and below worlds. In the natural world, I am reminded of the natural rhythm of all things. I am reminded of how Spirit is embodied in me and all around me.

Nature shows me how Spirit moves, dances, and sings in concert with all living beings. Spirit courses through all things. We are spiritual in nature. From this awareness we begin to practice vidya and move from a place of deep knowing and clear sight based on our connection with pure and higher consciousness. It is my belief this consciousness is meant to inform how we live our lives. From an awareness of higher consciousness, we can create less suffering for ourselves and others. Not just now but for the future. Vidya allows us to see the reality that could be and has already been seeded from the unbreakable bond between us and all things—collective liberation.

The practices that follow are intended to support you as you explore alignment with your Higher Self, pure consciousness, and right knowledge. They have been created to assist you in tapping into your inner wisdom as you work through the layers of conditioning that mask your true nature. These practices include reflection questions, asana, pranayama, meditation, mudra, and mantra.

REFLECTION QUESTIONS

▶ What is the importance of vidya to you? What does it mean to you to have clear sight?

▶ In what ways has the natural world brought you back to your own true nature? If you haven't yet had this experience, how might you engage the natural world to support you in remembering your true nature?

▶ What has gotten in the way of your ability to clearly see the divine spark and nature in yourself and others?

▶ What allows you to see the divine spark and nature in all beings?

▶ How does the ability to clearly see and practice right knowledge support us in creating conditions for collective liberation?

ASANA

This posture is intended to deepen your ability to clearly see and align with right knowledge and the absolute truths expressed through the practice and philosophy of yoga. You can practice the posture standing, seated in a chair, or on the ground. You might also decide to take the elements of this posture, and the postures offered in subsequent chapters, and explore a different variation of them, cultivating the same experience of the intention of the posture.

Tadasana, Mountain Pose

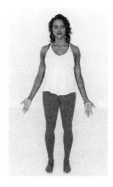

Mountain pose is a posture where you can explore steadiness and strength and a deep connection to the earth. In my experience, it cultivates a sense of staying steady amid chaos or things that might cloud one's judgment or field of experience. To me, this pose embodies the steadiness we must cultivate as we work toward connecting to our wisdom and radiant light.

Standing Variation of Mountain Pose

You can stand on the earth or on a mat. Mountain pose can be practiced with your feet hip distance apart or toes together. To align your body in mountain pose, take a moment to position your hips over your ankles, torso over your hips, and shoulders over your torso; move your shoulders back and down, and extend your arms down by your side with your hands open and fingers pointing toward the earth. Allow the center of your body to align by moving your pel-vis to center, not too far forward or too far back. You don't want to overtuck your tailbone or stick your buttocks out too far. Try to find middle ground here. Reach up with the crown of your head and press down into the earth with your feet. Once you have found mountain pose, either close your eyes or leave them open with a soft gaze and take a few deep breaths. Breathe in steadiness and clear sight, and feel your connection to the earth.

Seated Variation of Mountain Pose

You can practice this in a chair or on the earth. If you are practicing this posture in a chair, take a seat and place your feet on the ground or onto blocks to bring the earth to you. Align your torso over your hips, and you can either allow your arms to extend down toward the earth or rest your hands on your knees, palms facing up or down. Relax your shoulders back and down, and reach up through the crown of your head. Take a few deep breaths here. If you are seated on the earth, you might choose to elevate your hips with a blanket or pillow.  Once you have found your seat, you can rest your hands on your knees with your palms facing up or down. Allow your shoulders to relax back and down, and extend up through the crown of your head. Take a few deep breaths.

Pranayama ——————————————————————

You can combine this pranayama practice with the meditation that follows, or you can practice it as an individual practice. For this practice, you will move through

Pran Vidya

Pran Vidya is a pranayama practice that is believed to bring wisdom to us through conscious breathing. You will explore breath retention for this practice, which requires you to hold your breath for a period of time before exhaling. If breath retention makes you feel as if you cannot breathe or that you are restricted in some way, please shorten the time of retention or simply breathe in and out.

Find a comfortable way to be in your body.

Place your hands on your knees with your palms facing up or down.

Close your eyes, or find a soft gaze on the ground in front of you.

Begin by taking a few deep breaths, feeling the breath fill your body and release from your body.

After you've taken a few deep breaths, breathe in for a count of four, hold your breath for four counts, and then empty for four counts. After three rounds of this, increase the counts per inhale, the time you retain the breath, and counts per exhale to six counts. Then eight counts for each.

This way of breathing has the power to generate more life force and pull down various truths from the universal consciousness.

If you want to increase the counts even more over time, you can, up to twenty counts per inhale and exhale as well as the time you retain the breath.

After you have completed this pranayama practice, slowly breathe in and out and take your time to come back into your space.

Take a moment to notice what consciousness you have gained from the practice.

MEDITATION

This meditation is focused on cultivating clear sight about your true nature. I will invite you to connect to your own experience of breathing and then to the collective experience of breathing. If you want to practice this meditation outside, feel free, as it will be easier for you to connect to nature spirits and feel the pure consciousness embodied within nature spirits and the ecosystem.

If you prefer to stay inside, you can certainly move through this meditation indoors and in the comfort of your space.

Clear Sight and True Nature Meditation

Find a comfortable way to be in your body—seated, lying down, or standing.

Once you have found your posture, and if you are seated, place your hands on your knees, the palms facing up or down. If you are standing, you might decide to place your arms by your side.

Close your eyes, or find a soft gaze on the ground in front of you.

Take a few deep breaths to ground and center yourself.

Begin to breathe more deeply, offering a deeper inhale and a longer exhale. Feel the flow of breath as it moves into your body and out of your body.

After several deep breaths, imagine all the other living beings in your space and outside of your space, inhaling and exhaling. Visualize all of the living beings around you. Visualize the rise and fall of their chests as they inhale and exhale. Visualize the sound of the breath. Visualize and even hear the sound of whales breathing through their blowholes, sea turtles coming up for air, the sound of a baby breathing, the sound of a furry companion breathing deeply, and the deep exhales and inhales of the earth—the deep breath moving through everyone and everything.

Stay here for a few minutes, breathing alongside everything and everyone in communion with all that can be felt when you tap into your radiant light and the truth of who you are, and the truth of pure consciousness in all things. All around.

When you are ready to move out of this meditation, move out of it slowly. Gently come back into your space and take some time to reorient, hopefully feeling a deeper connection to everything around you.

Mudra

You may be familiar with *Anjali* mudra, as many of us are often guided into this mudra at the beginning or end of an asana practice or meditation. Anjali mudra serves as a reminder that our practice is a prayer. It reminds us that everything we do is in service of something bigger than our own individual experience because of our connection with all living beings past and present. It represents the union of the individual self with the universal Self. As you work with this mudra, explore being able to see and feel your connection with all living things past and present, and move from a space of interconnectedness.

You can add this practice to the end of the asana shared above or practice it on its own.

Anjali Mudra

Find a comfortable way to be in your body.

Close your eyes, or find a soft gaze on the ground in front of you.

Place your hands on your knees with your palms facing up or down.

Take a few deep breaths to ground and center yourself.

Now bring your hands together and into heart center. Gently press your palms together, and feel the union of your palms and your thumbs coming into connection with your heart.

Take several deep breaths and feel the rise and fall of your chest and the way your heart and hands move as you breathe.

Feel how connected you are with your breath, your hands, your heart, and all things.

When you feel ready to move out of this posture, gently bow your head to your hands, honoring what is always true, your union with everything.

Release the mudra and take a few deep breaths and some time to reconnect to your space, carrying this feeling of connection with you as you move through the rest of your day.

MANTRA

Mantras originate from Hinduism and Buddhism. They are statements one repeats to oneself to deepen consciousness, and they aid in meditation. Traditionally, mantras were given to students by their teachers when they were initiated as a practitioner of spiritual practice or as a rite of passage. I have been given mantras from teachers but do not consider myself to be someone who can give a mantra to someone else. The lineage of yoga is one I have learned, not one that was directly passed on to me from India, its place of origin, and I am not in a position to pass mantras on to people as part of an initiation into a lineage or as a sign of one's deep commitment to the practice of yoga. I will offer mantras from my experience as a teacher and student. I have practiced with mantras for years now and work with them as sayings or statements that I repeat to myself to deepen awareness and affirm truths I am hoping to embody more fully.

The mantra I will offer here is both about clear sight and our connection to all things, everywhere.

You can repeat this mantra several times after or as part of your meditation practice.

I Am Connected Mantra

I am connected to all things everywhere. All that has ever been and will be. I am the oneness of all beings. The oneness I am.

It is my hope these practices will aid you in feeling the pure con-sciousness that resides within and around you. These practices will aid you in deepening your connection and gaining clear sight so you aren't afflicted by the illusion of our separation. None of what we experience exists in isolation; it is all connected.

Part Two

Asmita and Our Ego

Part Two explores the second klesha, asmita, or an overidentification with the ego. It explores how avidya is connected to asmita and how the belief that we are separate could lead us to overidentify with our ego to the point where we believe we are, and are driven by, ego. This section offers practices to explore what is beyond the ego as well as offers content about what a healthy relationship with the ego might look like.

4

Asmita

Enlightenment is ego's ultimate disappointment.

—CHÖGYAM TRUNGPA

I BEGAN PRACTICING YOGA over two decades ago. I have practiced with many teachers, some of whom had huge followings and some who had just a few students in their classes. I have learned something from each teacher I have studied with. After practicing yoga for some time, I decided to pursue yoga teacher training in order to deepen my practice and begin to infuse my psychotherapy work with yoga and other healing modalities. When I went through yoga teacher training in 2009, there was only one local yoga school offering training, unlike today, when there are 200-hour trainings everywhere. Now one doesn't have to look far for a certification to teach the vast and ancient practice of yoga.

When I completed my 200-hour training, I was eager to begin teaching in one of my favorite studios in town. I was offered the opportunity to teach a weekly class, and so I began teaching to the one or two students who would join me. Low class attendance went on for a while until I started to offer a free monthly community class. Students would flock to the free class, and over time, some of them began to attend my weekly class.

When I began to teach yoga, I remember feeling as if I was competing with seasoned teachers, and this didn't feel good to me. I would be in my room waiting for students to show up, next to another teacher's room that was full. I noticed that, at times, I felt jealous of other teachers. It wasn't that I thought of myself as an amazing teacher, but some part of me wanted what I witnessed other teachers having: a following. This desire to have a following wasn't rooted in a belief that I was the center of the universe. It is very natural to want to be seen as valid and credible. It is equally very natural and human to want others to see your worth. Even so, I didn't like the feeling of jealousy building inside me.

I believed I had something to offer, but so did the other teachers. Part of the tension for me was that I was one of only a few Black teachers at this studio, and I understood the industry of yoga and wellness had been whitewashed. I wanted to be seen as a valid and valuable teacher and to make an offering in that space. I was deeply committed to justice work and wanted to infuse some consciousness raising about how to create conditions for justice into my yoga practice and teaching. I knew there was a lack of representation of many groups in the industry of yoga—2SLGBTQIA+, disabled people, elders, larger-bodied folks, BIPOC (Black, Indigenous, and People of Color), and many other underrepresented groups.

On some level, I knew the practice of yoga isn't about how many people showed up in my class. I knew the practice of yoga isn't about my near-empty yoga room or the room full of students in my colleagues' classes. I knew the practice of yoga is about liberation and devoting our actions in service to something bigger than ourselves. Still, even as I understood these truths, I yearned to be seen as a good teacher or, at a minimum, as someone who could offer the teaching of yoga in a way that would create transformation for individuals and the collective.

By the time I left teaching at that studio, I was teaching a total of six classes in two studios in town. My classes were chock-full of students. I was known as a popular teacher, and I had a huge following. Of course, this felt good because I was offering something people wanted and desired, but again the practice of yoga isn't about the number of students we have. It is about coming into alignment with oneself so that one can live into their dharma and purpose on this planet in service of the collective good.

The Ego

Often we think of the ego as negative—for example, when someone holds a high opinion of themselves or is conceited. Egocentrism can look like someone acting as if they are the center of the universe and as if they aren't in relationship with other beings. It can look like taking up a lot of psychic, physical, and emotional space at the expense of others. Our egos can certainly get in our way and cause friction in our lives and in our relationships. But the ego itself isn't a bad thing. Our egos develop as part of a process of individuating from others, often our caretakers, so that we can develop an understanding of who we are and who we want to be.

In this next section, I will explore Sigmund Freud's psychoanalytic theory of personality. I first learned about Freud in college when I took a semester of abnormal psychology. Many things happened in that class, one of which was that I began to think everything I and others did was abnormal; this made me question what "normal" even is. The second thing that occurred is that I learned about many psychiatrists and researchers, including Freud, Jung, Skinner, and Adler. With Freud in particular, there was then, and continues to be now, a lot of skepticism about his theories and methodology. I will offer a few points from his personality theory because some of how he describes the ego and the different parts of who we are seems aligned with yogic philosophy, specifically what drives our decisions, how the mind turns, how we express and embody different qualities that make up our nature, and how the ego and an overidentification with ego creates suffering for us and others. The ego and who we believe ourselves to be—based on the mind and ego—affects our sense and perception of self and experience in the world.

Please read this section with full awareness that many of the so-called fathers of psychology were white-bodied or European cisgender men who had the clout and power to suggest that they fully understood how our minds work and how our personalities develop. They had the power to create theories about the mind and our psychology because of their proximity to social and institutional power, which is a concept we will explore in the next chapter related to the ego and asmita. Each of the "fathers of psychology" have contributed to the pathologization of many groups of people who are less proximal to power, including but not limited to BIPOC, bigger-bodied, and 2SLGBTQIA+ people. Unlike yoga philosophy, many of the psychological theories created by and shared with us from the "fathers of psychology" aren't rooted in any analysis about how social and institutional power operate, or in spiritual practice or the reality that we are all spiritual beings. In this way, they differ from yoga philosophy. Still, it can be helpful for us to be reminded about how the ego might be structured. After this section, I will go on to explore more yoga philosophy and share a bit about how it differs from Freud's personality theory.

Psychological theories, including Freud's psychoanalytic theory about personalities, posit that there are three different parts to the ego: id, ego, and superego. Freud suggested id is present when we are born and is based on meeting our instinctual needs and desires. This part of the ego is unconscious and connected to the most primitive part of the personality, including our biological needs and reflexes. You can consider a baby's need for touch, food, warmth, and some sort of soothing response when they feel distressed as their needs and reflexes. If a baby's needs aren't met, tension arises, and often a baby will cry as a way of letting their caretaker know they need something or that a need hasn't been met. This is id, and a baby's need for survival often means they are driven by this part of their ego. Over time, many of us individuate from our caretakers and learn to meet our own needs. In addition, we learn self-soothing techniques and distress tolerance skills to come back into balance when our needs aren't or haven't been met.

Being driven by id for the whole of our lives would mean being driven by our needs and desires and operating from a place of distress when our needs and desires aren't met. We do not always truly need what we desire. A practice of discernment and self-discipline is meant to support us in assessing the difference between true needs and desires, or wants. We will explore more about desire in part three, which focuses on raga, attachment to pleasure, and part four, which focuses on dvesha, aversion or avoidance. What I will share now is an example of id and how it can lead people, especially those more proximal to power, to want to maintain their power and not to see their desire for power as deriving from their ego and the ways they are rewarded by dominant culture and systems of power for striving for more power. We live in a system of capitalism that only allows a small percentage of people to thrive financially and creates financial, emotional, mental, spiritual, and physical suffering for others. The 1 percent who is most proximal to power due to class status may be ruled by a desire to have as many financial resources as possible even if it means others will suffer. The 1 percent is upholding the ideal that more is better and making it seem as if greediness is an acceptable behavior. Of course, this flies in the face of *aparigraha*, which teaches us to practice greedlessness, and truly assess what we need as we understand how resources are inequitably allocated as well as the impact this has on those less proximal to class privilege.

The second part of the personality presented in Freud's psychoanalytic personality theory is ego. He believed that ego derives from id and that our desires and impulses need some part of the personality to keep them in check. This part of the ego works with id to meet our needs and desires in ways that require us to be more discerning about what we truly need. This part of the personality engages the process of rational thinking to support us in problem-solving and self-discipline. "The ego operates at conscious, preconscious, and unconscious levels."[7] When Freud first presented the personality theory about ego, he was referring to ego as a sense of self, but this theory later suggested that ego is also connected to our cognitions and behaviors, including judgment, self-regulation, and self-discipline.

The superego is the final part of the personality and is connected to our moral compass. This part of the ego supports us in understanding and taking action from a place of what is right or wrong. Often our learning around what is right and wrong, and our values and beliefs, are heavily influenced by our environment growing up—by our community, and by how we are shaped and socialized. The superego continues to grow over time and thus our values can change based on how our consciousness shifts.

As shared in chapter 1, avidya is about ignorance, and we experience it when we confuse our true self, pure consciousness, with ego. This causes us to get caught up in the fluctuations of the mind. This experience can make it difficult to develop awareness of ourselves and to discern who we are outside of our bodies, sensations, and thoughts. One of the obstacles on the path of yoga that creates suffering is *ahamkara*, meaning ego or a sense of "I-ness." We can overidentify with "I-ness" to the point that it is all we think we are. Asmita and ahamkara are closely related in that ahamkara describes the ego, and asmita is the overidentification with the ego. Asmita refers to the way we suffer because we overidentify with some part of who we believe we are. This causes us to lose sight of who we truly are. Asmita comes from confusing our identities with the whole of who we are.

> Asmita arises from the apparent oneness of the power of the perceiver and the power of perception.
> —YOGA SUTRA 2.6, TRANSLATED BY PANDIT RAJMANI TIGUNAIT IN
> *THE PRACTICE OF THE YOGA SUTRA: SADHANA PADA*

Asmita surfaces when consciousness—the perceiver—mistakenly identifies itself with the tools it uses to perceive the objects. The mind is the tool. For example, if I perceive I am all of the roles I fill—worker, daughter, partner, friend, activist, author, educator, etc.—and this is all of who I am because of my mind's perception, this doesn't allow me to see myself beyond the roles I inhabit. These roles shape my experience in the world, but I am not solely these roles or what is associated with them by dominant culture or systems. Yoga Sutra 2.6 describes the way we mistake the whole of our identity as only what the mind perceives. We will delve into this more deeply in chapter 5.

When I first started teaching, I identified as both a new teacher and a student. This identity was important to me, and at times I sought validation for this part of my identity from how many students would show up for my yoga class. In my mind, validation of this part of my identity equated to how many people would attend my classes. To take this further, how many people attended my class was then equated with whether or not I was a good teacher, by my own standards and the standards of the industry of yoga and wellness. These thoughts, and equating who I truly am and my value with the number of students in my class, took me away from the true intention of why I started down the path of yoga in the first place.

When I would feel upset or jealous that students didn't show up to my class while other teachers had full rooms, at times, I would forget why I became a yoga teacher. When I was sulking about one student instead of ten students showing up, I was unable to focus on the gifts I could offer to that one student who chose to practice with me and the gifts I could receive from my interaction with them. When I was complaining about other teachers and curious about what they had that I didn't have, I wasn't practicing yoga. I was practicing comparison, which for me never leads me to a positive place and always moves me away from intention and dharma, my purpose.

I confused the truth of who I am, which is a spiritual being whose spirit is more vast than any amount of students who might attend a particular yoga class and a person who is deeply committed to a path of liberation, with material things in the world—in this case, how many people might attend my class. I confused the truth of who I am, which is someone who wants to devote her life's work to something bigger than herself, with the business of yoga—you must have X amount of students to be seen as valid and valuable and be a "successful" yoga teacher. We begin to overidentify with parts of our identity, we begin to experience separation, and we forget the core of who we are, the soul, atman.

I became a yoga teacher to understand more about the ancient practice of yoga. The practice of yoga has provided healing for me and transformed my life in many ways. I wanted to take this transformation and inspire others to transform in my classes and in the world. I became a yoga teacher because I believed the spiritual path of yoga very clearly outlines a pathway toward liberation. I became a yoga teacher because of a yearning to devote my actions to something bigger than myself and a desire to remember how vast my spirit is. If you are a yoga or spiritual practitioner, I invite you to take a moment to connect with why you practice yoga or are devoted to a spiritual path. After you have gained some clarity about why you practice yoga or are devoted to a spiritual path, ask yourself how your practice and path affect how you show up for yourself, in relationships with other beings, and in the world. How does your practice of yoga and spiritual practice connect with how and why you do whatever it is you do in the world? The questions above are meant to support you in better understanding "your why," as my friend Stephanie

Ghoston Paul says, for what you are doing. What we do needs to be connected to something bigger than our identities and egos.

There is an overlap between Freud's personality theory and yoga philosophy. Both speak about the ego and how, when we overidentify with who we believe ourselves to be based on our identities, this can cause us to operate out of impulses and be driven by our desires. This behavior may not be in the best interest of ourselves or the collective. Just as Freud's theory suggests that different parts of the ego, id, and the superego develop to help us begin to practice discernment and learn more about how we want to show up in the world—beyond our egos, what we desire, and our impulses—in the Yoga Sutras, Patanjali offers that our self-image can be driven by the desire to hold on to certain attributes and identities. The process of developing self-concept and self-image and our identification with certain parts of who we are can become concretized in a way that makes everything else seem meaningless. Our self-image is then placed at the center of the universe, and we can expect the rest of the world to revolve around it. This is why the Yoga Sutras offer practices to support us in recognizing who we are beyond the ego, practices meant to bring us closer to *brahma-bhava*, "the all pervading experience of consciousness instead of *jiva bhava*, or *asmita*, the limited sense of individuality."[8]

> Asmita (I-am-ness, strong self-identification). We hold our self-image so dear that it overshadows the existence of our core being, the soul. The function of asmita is subtle and yet extremely potent. To a seeker not armed with the highest level of vigilance, asmita is like a black hole that can devour the brilliance of a thousand suns.
> —YOGA SUTRA 2.6, TRANSLATED BY PANDIT RAJMANI TIGUNAIT IN *THE PRACTICE OF THE YOGA SUTRA: SADHANA PADA*

As explained earlier in the chapter, the ego in itself isn't a bad thing. What causes suffering is the way the ego gets in the way of us realizing the fullness of who we are. Asmita limits our worldview. The practice of yoga expands our worldview. I needed some level of ego to begin a practice of yoga, a sense of self that wanted to expand her understanding of Spirit and spiritual practice. When I felt called to deepen my practice and offerings to my psychotherapy clients, this required a sense of self and ego as well. This is what drove me to go to teacher training. The decision to pursue yoga teacher training came from my sense of self and a desire to be in alignment with teaching about the mind and body as I supported my clients in coming into wholeness. If I had not thought that I could help people or be of service in some way, I wouldn't have attended social work school. If I hadn't believed I had something to share to advance a conversation and practice of understanding the intersection of yoga and justice, I wouldn't have created a body of work called Skill in Action. There are countless examples of risks I wouldn't have taken or opportunities I wouldn't have pursued had it not been for my ego. It is when our egos are out of balance or when we overidentify with our work, occupation, and identities that we suffer.

REFLECTION QUESTIONS

Please take a moment to reflect on the following reflection questions:

- ▶ How has your ego and sense of self supported you in pursuing opportunities in your life?

- ▶ In what ways do you experience yourself becoming overidentified with certain parts of your identities or who you believe yourself to be?

- ▶ What do you notice when you overidentify with particular identities you embody?

- ▶ How might you maintain a strong sense of self and an awareness of your identities while holding on to the vision of yourself as someone with an expanded worldview and consciousness?

As explored in chapter 1, all of the kleshas are connected, and asmita arises from avidya, ignorance. Just as believing we are separate from one another and forgetting we are interconnected causes suffering, developing our sense of self based on the belief that we are separate from all beings also causes suffering. This samskara rooted in ego, perception, and thoughts causes us to lose sight of ourselves as pure consciousness. This causes us to forget the everlasting nature of our existence and soul. In the next chapter, we will continue to explore asmita as it relates to identities and social location and the social and institutional power we are assigned because of the identities we embody. The next chapter will provide nuance to the experience of asmita and is intended to provide a layer of complexity and understanding related to how we experience the relative truth that we are in our human bodies as we navigate systems and structures that have created a hierarchy of bodies.

> We are accustomed to living in a world defined by and confined to the forces of time, space, and the law of cause and effect. Our deep familiarity with ourselves as limited entity makes embracing our limitless self extremely distressing. We prefer becoming "big" in our familiar little world to losing ourselves in the vastness of our pure consciousness.
> —Pandit Rajmani Tigunait, *The Practice of The Yoga Sutra: Sadhana Pada*

5

Asmita, Power, and Privilege

Like our lived yoga practices, intersectionality allows us to step out of perceived and socially constructed binaries to hold the full spectrum of experience and move into conscious action to create social change.
—ANUSHA WIJEYAKUMAR AND MELANIE KLEIN,
"WHAT IS INTERSECTIONALITY IN YOGA AND WHY DOES IT MATTER?"
YOGA JOURNAL, JULY 31, 2022

OFTEN WHEN I facilitate racial equity or Skill in Action train-ings, I share with the group that the most salient identity I embody is Blackness. I am a Black American who has only lived in the US. In this country, white supremacy—the belief system and ide-ology that being white and whiteness is superior and that being Black, Indigenous, and People of Color (BIPOC) is inferior—permeates every aspect of culture. White supremacy has shaped cultural norms and prac-tices, our values, who we believe holds value, and belief systems about who—based on the identities they embody—is superior and inferior. White supremacy has also influenced our institutions, such as health-care, wellness, housing, banking, the educational system, and the like. It has shaped institutional communication practices, how we relate to timelines, and what behaviors, clothing, and hairstyles are considered professional. It has definitely shaped my sense of self, how the world sees me, and how I see and view the world.

Avidya limits our ability to see clearly and makes us forget who we indeed are. Clear sight isn't solely about seeing our true nature. It is also about seeing patterns that are playing out related to power and how power functions and influences our human experience in the earthly realm. These patterns relate to asmita in that the negative patterns of separation and polarization are often based on the constructed identities that dominant culture has created for us. Based on my Blackness and how white supremacy operates, I understand how white power works and where it positions me based on my race. I can see how power is centralized in the hands of those—in this example, white-bodied people—most proximal to power because of the identities they embody. I am often marginalized because of race, which has allowed me to understand how marginalization works and how it is happening to others who are less proximal to power based on the identities they embody. I share my experience of being Black with groups because, even though I understand it doesn't define the whole of who I am, it does shape my experience in the world. Just as being a cisgender woman shapes my experience in the world. Just as my being middle class shapes how I move through the world. Just as being an American citizen shapes how I navigate the U.S. and other countries.

As we explored in chapter 4, asmita occurs when we overidentify with the ego or some part of our identity. This chapter investigates how our experience of identity (our race, gender and gender expression, class status, education level, body size and shape, citizenship status, profession, etc.) influences our sense of self and might contribute to strongly identifying with a part of who we are. Chapter 5 explores how a strong connection to an identity might further the separation and polarization we are experiencing in the collective and world at this time. This chapter looks at how we might overidentify with a particular part of our identity because it feels most salient to our relative experience on earth as we navigate systems and hierarchies.

All my embodied identities have shaped me, and to some degree, they have shaped how I see and experience myself and others. As I share the concept of social location and social and institutional power in this chapter, I will ask you to hold at least two truths. The first is that the identities you embody shape your experience of yourself and others—the identities you embody shape the choices you make, your belief system and values, and the actions you take in the world. The second truth I will ask you to hold is that you are a spiritual being. Often, systems of power and resulting marginalization can interfere with the reality that we are living in the earthly realm, we are impacted by earthly conditions, and we are also spiritual beings. I have a spiritual practice and am on a spiritual path, and I understand I am an extension of Spirit, and Spirit resides inside and around me. This is true. Even so, there is no way for me to transcend Blackness or any other identity people within the earthly realm have constructed for me. This is also true. I am not only a spiritual being but also a human being.

In large part, asmita and all of the kleshas are related to prakriti, our nature. But our nature and mental and physical tendencies, self-perception, and perception of the world are influenced by the outer world and our socialization. Asmita, I-amness, which derives from an overidentification with one or more than one part of ourselves, intersects with how ego has influenced power structures such that some people truly believe their identities are superior to others. For example, I have been shaped to believe that because I am non-disabled at this time in my life, I am somehow superior to disabled people. This isn't what I consciously believe about myself but what I have internalized from dominant culture and institutions. I have been socialized to believe that spaces are designed for my abled body, and in large part, they are. I don't need a wheelchair ramp, a parking space closer to the building, or access to a riding cart when I visit the grocery store. I don't have to consider whether or not my voice will be heard in a space because of my abilities. Often it is. Based on my abilities, I am read as competent and as someone who can make choices for herself. The culture is set up for my abled body. If I am not in constant interrogation about what this means, I might begin to internalize that I am entitled to have my needs met in a particular way. I could begin to think that everyone is having the same experience as I am. I might begin to believe I am better than or separate from disabled communities. On a large scale, this is what has created our ableist culture and the hierarchical patterns of ableism that permeate every part of culture. These patterns are based on misperception because, in truth, I am not superior to disabled individuals. And still, dominant culture tells me that I am.

This is just one example of how what we internalize from dominant culture, based on the identities it has constructed for us and those we embody, can lead to an overidentification with a part of our identity, and thus lead us to believe we are separate because we are superior to someone else. If we are not in constant interrogation of our socialization and internalizations, then we risk creating a samskara based on a hierarchy of identity. Hierarchies of identities have created institutional samskaras and shaped cultural samskaras based on the idea that one group can be better than another. Patterns that emerge from these hierarchies include but aren't limited to greed, stealing, land theft, cultural appropriation, power hoarding, and silencing the voices of those less proximal to power while simultaneously uplifting the voices of people who are more proximal to power. These patterns have become embedded in our systems, structures, institutions and have shaped cultural norms and how we relate to one another. These embedded tendencies and patterns are set up to cater to those more proximal to power. For example, the industry of yoga in the West caters to thin, non-disabled, cisgender, young, white-bodied, heterosexual women. Another example: the government bailed out banks and large corporations while low-wealth and poor folks struggled to make ends meet. Institutions routinely provide ease to those of us more proximal to power instead of addressing the needs of those who are less proximal to power. These systems maintain and sustain themselves because those more proximal to social and institutional power have created a world that does not have to account for the ways it isn't addressing the needs of those who are less proximal to power.

Social Location

> All people have a social location that is defined by their gender, race, social class, age, ability, religion, sexual orientation, and geographic location. Each group membership confers a certain set of social roles and rules, power, and privilege (or lack of), which heavily influence our identity and how we see the world.
> —BRIANNE BENNESS, "SOCIAL LOCATION, WHAT PEOPLE MEAN," *MEDIUM*, OCTOBER 12, 2017

Below, I will offer a framework to understand social location—a tool we can use to explore how overidentification with ego and identity has influenced our experience of the world, both our inner and outer worlds. In my first book, *Skill in Action: Radicalizing Your Yoga Practice to Create a Just World*, I shared about this framework as I invited readers to reflect on how we are uniquely positioned to make change through an assessment of our identities and proximity to power. After having shared this tool, I was introduced to the term *social location*, which is about our social group membership and identities. Social location encapsulates an analysis of power and helps us more clearly understand where we are each situated, based on how power is structured and based on our identities. It also points to our specific roles and responsibilities in regards to what we do with our social and institutional power. It is a framework that provides an overview of what is flawed and imbalanced because of how institutional, systemic, and cultural power has been structured. It invites us into a practice of accountability and solidarity with those who are less proximal to power. In this way, it invites us to consider our relationship with all beings. Social location invites us to move from a place of "I-amness" to a place of collective action. In chapter 6, I share practices designed to move us into action from a place of "we are" instead of "I am."

Below you will find a visual representation of social location—the wheel of power and privilege. There are a few caveats I would like to offer about this wheel.

Social Location Wheel

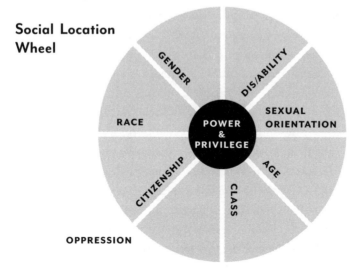

There are several versions of this wheel. The one used here is a simplified version of the wheel that lists just a few identities you might embody, with power and privilege in the center and the experience of oppression on the outer edges. This wheel isn't inclusive of all identities; it includes a blank spoke to represent that gap. As you reflect on asmita and your identities, you might enjoy creating your own wheel, and I will offer an invitation to do so later in this chapter. The social location wheel included here doesn't list the different identities within each category—for example, for class, we could look at different levels of class, including upper class, rich, the one percent, middle class, lower class, poor, underestimated, and so on. These aren't included, but you might choose to explore them in more detail if you create your own wheel. For race, different categories could include white, Latinx or Latine, Asian, South Asian, Indigenous, Black, and so on. And we could also list skin tone as a separate category, because often skin tone shapes our proximity to social and institutional power—if you are a light-skinned Person of Color, your experience is different from that of someone who is darker skinned or Black. This experience is a result of the way social and institutional power have been constructed and the way colorism functions in our culture, systems, and institutions.

The wheel doesn't speak to the whole of who we are, but it does offer an opportunity for you to reflect on your identities, where you have been placed, how you are positioned, and your perception because of your positionality to power. As we consider how asmita creates samskaras that limit our ability to be free, we can break down any of these identities and look at how they operate within culture and institutions, and we can identify how the construction of these identities was always intended to separate us from ourselves, one another, and our divinity. For the purposes of deepening your understanding of social location, I will share about one identity where I am more proximal to power and one where I am further away from power, in the margins of the circle. Then I will invite you to reflect on your experience by journaling in response to some questions about social location.

As mentioned before, I am Black. Based on how the racial hierarchy was constructed by white-bodied people, Black is at the bottom of the racial hierarchy, and white is at the top. Other groups of People of Color are between the two fixed points of white and Black. As mentioned earlier in this chapter, my Blackness feels most salient to me because we live in a culture that upholds white supremacy. This affects where I go and do not, opportunities afforded to me, people's perception of me based on what they have learned from various institutions and cultural norms, how safe or unsafe I feel, when my voice is centered or not, and really, so much of my life. My white-bodied friends and colleagues share with me that many of them have had to go through a learning process to understand their whiteness and how it affects them, their relationship with other white-bodied individuals, and with BIPOC. This learning process they reference isn't something I had to go through based on my racial identity. The world told me very clearly who I was based on race, Black. The world equated Blackness with criminality and unworthiness.

According to dominant culture, being Black means that I am in the furthest margins of the social location wheel. This is not how I think of myself, but it is part of my reality because the wheel places white-bodied individuals in the center of power and gives white-bodied individuals access to resources and decision-making power based on their racial identity. I do not mean to sound so binary. I do not believe all Black people have the same experience of marginalization, just as I do not believe all white-bodied individuals are afforded the same amounts of power. It is nuanced because all of the other identities listed in the wheel intersect with race. These intersections add layers of experience such that those of us with more points of oppression experience the compounding nature of these points moving us further and further away from power. And those of us who embody multiple points of privilege, whether or not we know it or are trained to believe it, are also having an experience where identities compound one another. Privilege upon privilege moves us closer to power.

In addition to being Black, I am non-disabled, which I described before. I benefit from our ableist culture and am given power because I am non-disabled. I experience privileges in the form of access to resources, space, and decision-making power because of this identity. And I am non-disabled and Black at the same time. While I experience marginalization due to my race, I experience the benefits of being more proximal to power because of my abilities.

I am going to ask you to take some time to reflect on questions about your identity. First, a reminder that, while I am asking you to reflect on your identities, they do not represent the full being you are. This is an opportunity for you to explore using the social location wheel to consider where you might overidentify with some part of who you are such that it creates obstacles in your life and the lives of others. It is an opportunity to reflect on these identities and how we relate to them, whether we claim them fully or whether we try to transcend or dismiss them, limiting our perception of who we truly are and can be.

First, begin by creating your own social location wheel. Please include the identities listed above and add any others that come to mind— you might add body size and shape, education level, language, mental health, housing, skin color, religion, and so on. Once you have created your wheel, please map your location by placing a dot where you might be located based on who has power and privilege and who does not. For me, for my race I would place a dot out near the margins, and for the dis/ability identity listed in the wheel I would place a dot in the center. For citizenship, I would place a dot in the center. For gender, I would place a dot close to the center but not in the center—I am a cisgender woman in a patriarchal society, and I am deeply affected by sexism. Those most marginalized by the construction of gender and how we express gender are nonbinary and transgender, whereas I am given more privilege and power because I am cisgender in a culture that uplifts cisgender as "normal." And because I am perceived as "normal" according to my gender, the culture says more power should be given to me. I am a woman affected by cisgender men—who would be in the center of this circle as far as the gender category—but I am not affected as negatively financially, emotionally, spiritually, psychically, or mentally as someone who is nonbinary or transgender. After you have mapped your location, take some time to look at the full map. Take a few deep breaths.

REFLECTION QUESTIONS ——————————————

Now, respond to the following reflection questions:

➤ How has your social location shaped your perception of yourself?

➤ Which identities do you embody that feel most salient to you?

➤ How has your social location shaped your perception of others who share your same identities?

➤ How has your social location shaped your perception of those who have different identities?

➤ How has what you have internalized from dominant culture about who you are based on the identities you embody affected your sense of self and ego?

➤ How has your social location affected your relationship with others who may be less proximal to social and institutional power?

➤ How has your social location and what you have internalized from dominant culture moved you away from your inherent divinity?

I invite you to take a few more deep breaths after you explore these prompts.

Knowing our social location provides an opportunity to understand why we and others suffer due to our proximity to power and how power has been structured. An awareness of our social location can help us better understand that we are not all having the same experience in this earthly realm, even as we are all spiritual and divine beings. To me, social location is a tool that can help us create conditions where our egos and desires drive fewer of our actions, especially if our ego and sense of self is based on what we have internalized from dominant culture about who we are. It is a tool for us to look at the imbalance in the world due to the imbalance of power. This imbalance of power reinforces ego and asmita by giving entire groups of people power and privilege and simultaneously taking power and privilege away from other groups of people. Because of power and dominant culture, and where these things have located us based on our identities, we have an opportunity to disrupt avidya and asmita, ignorance and "I-amness," or to continue to engage in patterns that keep these obstacles in place.

Earlier in this chapter, I mentioned the earthly realm and our experience in human bodies. Social location is something we experience because we are living worldly lives. We are human beings on the planet. Social location doesn't account for the fact that, while we have a specific social location, in any given moment or context, we are also spiritual in nature. We are spiritual beings. What this means to me is that my Blackness has shaped my experience, and white supremacy has created an earthly experience for me that is painful at times. And still, my Blackness also feels like part of what it means to be divine. Without it, I wouldn't be who I am. I fully and completely claim my Blackness as a gift from Spirit and my ancestors that has shaped who I am in the world—not the part of the social location wheel that points to the way I am marginalized but what exists beyond the wheel because of the clarity that I came from Spirit and embody Spirit now. A social location wheel and the very real circumstances and expressions of power and hierarchy will not take this away from me.

Earlier I invited you to reflect on a question about what you have internalized from dominant culture and how this has moved you further away from your divinity. Now I invite you to reflect on the identities you fully claim and feel pride in and ponder how these identities bring you closer to your divinity and to Spirit. In addition, I invite you to connect with the part of you that is not the social location wheel—the part that is more vast than the construct of a wheel to describe who you and we are. What does this feel like? How does it feel to allow yourself to connect with this part of who you are? What practices will not only support you in understanding social location and your experience as a human with various identities but also connect you to the part of you that is beyond or cannot be contained by the social location wheel?

In chapter 6, I will provide practices to guide you to this part of yourself, the true Self. I will explore how remembering our inherent divinity can move us closer to solidarity, wholeness, and alignment with Spirit. For now, I invite you to consider what the Yoga Sutras and the Bhagavad Gita offer us, which include two truths—we are living a worldly life, and our true nature is Spirit.

What will support you in remembering and holding both of these truths?

6

From I to We

The grasses feed the ants with seeds and the ants feed
the grasses with soil. They hand off life to one another.
They understand their interconnections; they understand
that the life of one is dependent on the life of all.
—ROBIN WALL KIMMERER, *BRAIDING SWEETGRASS: INDIGENOUS
WISDOM, SCIENTIFIC KNOWLEDGE, AND THE TEACHINGS OF PLANTS*

AS I SHARED in chapter 3, the natural world has offered salve to my
heart many times over. After having sat in awe of the natural
world and its way of cyclical working so many times, I've experienced the most wonder thus far by watching and learning about honeybees and their hives. I have not encountered any other organism
quite like the superorganism of a honeybee hive, although I know many
exist—ants, termites, wasps, thrips, aphids, and more. Although I am
sure aphids and termites could teach me some lessons about the power
of being a superorganism, I've spent most of my time with honeybees
learning profound lessons about nature and our collective well-being.
There is something about viewing a honeybee hive from the outside
as bees bring resources into the hive—pollen, nectar, and water—and
seeing, hearing, and smelling the inner workings of a hive that has
deepened my understanding of what it means to truly see and feel our
inherent connection to all things and beings everywhere. Being called
back into my inherent connection to all things has been an integral part

of recognizing when I am operating from a place of ego or "I-amness" versus acting from a place of "we-areness."

I don't recall what made me become a beekeeper other than a dream that led me to order all I needed to tend bees without ever having taken a beekeeping class and without the proper preparation, if there is such a thing, to be in relationship with the honeybee and the hive. Even though I am unclear about what exactly led me to the honeybee, or it to me, I am certain I am supposed to be in relationship with them to learn more about interconnectedness and to teach and share lessons learned about how truly interdependent we are as creatures big and small. When the bees arrived, I understood I was in relationship with them. But knowing one is in connection with something or someone, and learning how to listen, create balance in the relationship, practice reciprocity, and master interspecies communication takes time. I longed to have a magical, easeful relationship with the honeybees, one full of mystery and honeybee communication through dreams, telepathy, and more, but the beginning of tending bees didn't feel this way to me. Not at all.

The first few months of having bees on my land offered me a steep learning curve. I believe I was, and at times still am, working through a fear of the honeybees. At the same time, I was intrigued by how mysterious everything they did seemed and felt to me. I imagine that, at times, fear and mystery make a beautiful pairing, but when it comes to honeybees, I am not sure this pairing bodes well for a fruitful relationship. For the first season of tending bees, I remember approaching them with less care than they required because of my fear and lack of knowledge. They could smell and sense my fear from far away, well before I would make my way from my home through the yard to their hives. I am sure they could feel my lack of knowledge based on how clumsy I could be in the hive as I looked to make sure there were eggs—a sign of a laying queen, nectar to make honey for food for the hive, and pollen—a sign they were foraging for resources that would allow them to make bee bread, which is a vital resource for the worker bees and larvae.

Over time, I took a few online honeybee courses, read many practical and mystical books about honeybees, watched countless YouTube videos about how to tend the hive, and learned a bit more about the mystery of the honeybee. I learned techniques to support me in remaining calm when honeybees were flying around my head or bumping into me because they wanted me to close up their hive and leave. I learned more about listening to their vibration and the pitch at which they were humming. I learned about the actions humans take that disrupt the harmony of the hive. Over the past few years, I've learned so much about honeybees, from the honeybees themselves and from bee priestesses and beekeepers who wouldn't claim priesthood but would claim to be a bit more pragmatic in their beekeeping practices. I have learned more about this living superorganism that not only includes the honeybee itself but every part of the hive, from the honeybee to honeycomb to propolis to nectar to honey to brood to bee bread.

In chapter 4, I shared about the second klesha, asmita, and how it can lead to suffering not only for oneself but the collective because of how asmita creates separation from oneself and one's true nature due to an overidentification with ego. In chapter 5, I shared about the nuance of asmita, given that systems and cultural norms have been put in place that lead us to overidentify with embodied identities while moving us away from our inherent divinity and connection to all beings. In this chapter, the honeybee hive serves as a teacher, offering a few out of countless lessons for how we move away from an egoic state that causes suffering and separation and back into alignment with the Higher Self so we can be of service to something bigger than ourselves and, ultimately, suffer less. The honeybees serve as a guide to remind us of how we move from a place of "I-amness" to a place of "we-areness."

Devotion

The hum of a honeybee hive is one unified hum. Honeybees do not think of themselves as a single bee but rather as an extension of the hive. They do not act alone, and everything they do is in service of the hive and for the purpose of the sustenance and survival of the hive. When I learned about the devotion an individual honeybee holds for their entire hive, I was struck by and moved to observe all the ways this devotion showed up in acts of service in the hive. I knew there was something we could learn about remembering our connection to all beings and service from the honeybee.

Role

Each honeybee has a specific role, be that a worker or nurse bee, a guard bee, an undertaker, a heater bee in winter, a forager, or a queen. Each bee knows its role, but bees are believed to be able to revert back to a previous role if that is what the hive needs at the time. Honeybee hives go through different seasons tied to the resources around them and the changing temperatures in their region. In the spring through early summer, hives birth new generations and flourish, almost bursting at the seams with new life and energy. In the fall, they begin preparing to weather winter, and the queen stops laying eggs for a little while as the bees backfill the brood chamber with honey so they have enough food to make it through the winter.

Survival

The wisdom inherent in a honeybee hive, passed on from one generation of bees to the next, allows them to know what to do to survive. This is not to say they always do but to acknowledge the wisdom they embody that allows them to do all they can to put conditions in place to survive. Humans, and our effect on the rapid pace at which the climate is changing and the planet is heating up, coupled with commercial beekeeping practices contribute to the changing environmental conditions that have led to colony collapse and the plight of the honeybee. The plight of the honeybee isn't theirs to face alone; it is our plight, too. In fact, their plight mirrors the plight of humans and our ecosystem. We, too, are facing collapse, and in large part, this is due to the belief that we are separate and due to an overidentification with ego and individualism. This impending collapse is also due to the structures and systems mentioned and explored in chapter 5, which actively work to separate us from ourselves, one another, and nature.

If honeybees collapse, so do we. When one of us, human or honeybee, isn't thriving because we believe we are separate—too attached to our egos and our needs and desires that we are willing to risk collective care for individual or personal gain—none of us thrive. I am not exactly sure how honeybees became superorganisms or practitioners of collective care, but I do know honeybees derived from solitary bees. Evolution led them from solitary beings to communal hives that center and practice collective care. Perhaps this evolution was for their survival as a species. Perhaps it is to mirror to us what we must do to survive and create conditions where future generations and our planet can thrive. Honeybees had to evolve over time, just as we have done and must do.

The wisdom I have learned about commitment to one's hive from the honeybees could fill a book of its own. Here, I will share some about how the wisdom offered to us by the honeybees intersects with some of the wisdom, knowledge, and sweetness offered to us in the Yoga Sutras and Bhagavad Gita.

> The antidote to *asmita* is to remember that we're a tiny blip in the grand scheme, but an integral piece in the order of the cosmos.
> —GABRIELLE HOPP, "KLESHAS: THE FIVE AFFLICTIONS,"
> FEBRUARY 11, 2016, WWW.GABRIELLEHOPPYOGA.COM

The Cosmic Unfolding and Order

Both the Bhagavad Gita and Patanjali's Yoga Sutras share that we are something other than our bodies, minds, and senses. Both texts explore the danger of overidentifying with our bodies, minds, and senses because each one of these things changes over time. These texts invite us to journey back to our true Self, which is an extension of Spirit and all things. Given that we exist beyond our bodies, minds, and senses, these texts call us to understand both that a cosmic plan is unfolding and that we are part of the cosmic plan. In chapter 11 of the Bhagavad Gita, Krishna shares his cosmic form with Arjuna, which causes Arjuna to feel afraid because he realizes Krishna is the lord of all things—death, life, birth, and destruction. Arjuna comes to realize through guidance from Krishna that not only is there a larger cosmic plan unfolding, one Krishna is in charge of, but that Arjuna himself and Arjuna's dharma is part of this plan. The pathway to self-realization for Arjuna is devoting his actions to Krishna.

The Yoga Sutras urge us to practice trustful surrender, devoting our actions to God with the awareness we are part of God and the divine plan unfolding. This trustful surrender is infused in so many of the specific sutras that call us to practice various parts of the eight-limbed path to move toward self-realization. These lessons feel resonant for me and mirror so many of the lessons I've learned from the honeybees about Spirit, devotion, trustful surrender, and the cosmic plan we and the honeybees are part of. In many mystical traditions and stories, honeybees are said to be able to communicate between realms, the spiritual and physical realms. Honeybees are referred to as deeply mystical in Egyptian, African, South Asian, and Greek mythology and have been revered as divine beings. I believe they understand the cosmos in a way that the human mind cannot.

If you sit next to a honeybee hive and listen to the hum, you will recognize their divinity and your own. You will feel the cosmos through their vibratos and altos. You will recognize the sound of *aum*, which is said to be the sound of the universe. Part of what has made us lose our way is that we have forgotten we are part of a cosmic plan. We seem untethered to the reality that we are here as earthly beings but part of the cosmos and a cosmic order that is unfolding. I am not in the mind of a honeybee, but as I have watched and listened to them over time, it seems to me that, without a doubt, they understand they are part of a cosmic plan. They are aware of their existence both as a honeybee hive and as spiritual beings. This awareness allows them to act from a place that is much more connected to a larger and collective Self than the ego or a lower self. When we become wrapped up in what we do or the ego such that we cannot see outside of ourselves, what manifests is suffering due to a lack of remembering we are part of a larger whole. We must remember that our lives are a small part of a much larger picture that is unfolding right now—one that we will not see the beginning or end to, but one we are an essential part of. We must define and remember our place in the universe or we will feel wayward in our lives. We must also see our connection to all things; all things have a place in the universe and the cosmic unfolding.

The Yoga Sutras provide many practices, including meditation, devotion to and being in service of something bigger than ourselves, discipline, and trustful surrender to respond to our egos and the ways we foster our own suffering and are experiencing suffering. These practices allow us to come into union with ourselves and all things, moving into alignment with the universe. While I don't know if the honeybees know about the Yoga Sutras, I do know they are disciplined in the actions they take to support the hive. I know they are devoted not only to the hive but also to the larger ecosystem beyond their hive. They are benevolent in nature, but nature isn't always kind to them. I believe there must be some trustful surrender as they live out their dharma as part of the cosmic unfolding. We, too, must figure out what our roles are at this time of turmoil and chaos. From our social location and the moment and what it is calling for, we must figure out how to take mindful action from the larger Self because of our inherent divinity and because of what is at stake if we do not take mindful action from the larger Self—our humanity. The Bhagavad Gita points to dharma and illustrates what happens when we resist our karmic path. While we are, in fact, a tiny blip in the long arc of the cosmic unfolding, we all have a role to play in decreasing the collective suffering that is currently happening on our planet.

We must remember we are an extension of a larger whole, just as the honeybees do. We are not free-floating agents who are aimlessly moving through the atmosphere. We are in deep connection with one another. In my experience, as I take action in the world in service of the larger Self because I remember I am part of something bigger than myself, my actions support the collective. When I forget the larger Self, which happens all of the time because of my mind, ego, desires, samskaras, and what I cannot know or do not remember or see, my actions can certainly create conditions to support me, but at times, they can also harm or create suffering for others. So often, I want us to be like the honeybees, always thinking of the larger Self and what our divinity versus our egos is calling us to do. The practices offered in this chapter are not only meant to move us closer to our divinity and Spirit but also intended to move us away from an orientation focused on the ego and individualism and toward an orientation focused on the larger Self and collective. These practices are intended to support you as you learn to recognize samskaras that emerge from asmita, and to begin to break through the suffering that arises because of asmita.

REFLECTION QUESTIONS

Take a moment to reflect on the following reflection questions:

▶ In what ways have you been operating from an individualistic orientation versus an orientation focused on the collective?

▶ What is the risk of maintaining an egoic state focused on you as an individual?

▶ What are the benefits to us all of working toward an orientation that is about devotion to the collective and larger Self, which is connected to Spirit and the divinity within all?

▶ How do the teachings of yoga that you have learned and worked with in your life thus far direct you back to your Higher or larger Self?

ASANA

This posture is intended to allow you to connect to your heart space and the reality that you are something bigger than your body, mind, sense, ego, and desires. You can practice the posture standing, seated in a chair, or on the ground. You might also decide to take the elements of this posture and the postures offered in subsequent chapters and practice a different variation of them, cultivating the same experience of the intention of the posture.

Cactus Arms

Cactus arms allow the heart to open and for a connection to be felt with something bigger than oneself. In my experience, this physical expression can cultivate a sense of connection from my heart to all that is around me. This pose embodies the heartful work we must do to break through our egos and the suffering the ego can cause us—to remember we are bigger than the human body; we are Spirit.

Standing Variation of Cactus Arms

You can stand on the earth or on a mat. Find mountain pose, the pose offered in chapter 3. Once you have found mountain pose, either close your eyes or leave them open and take a few deep breaths, breathing in steadiness and clear sight and feeling your connection to the earth. As you feel ready, inhale, sweeping your arms up overhead. As you sweep your arms out and up overhead, you might begin to feel your connection to that which is around you—the people, plants, air, elements, energies, etc. Once your arms are overhead, bend your elbows and make cactus arms. Your palms can face forward as you open your heart and draw your shoulder blades together. Take three deep breaths. Notice your front and back body. Notice the opening happening across your chest. Open to Spirit and feel the expansive nature of your own spirit. Open to what is available from the heart and beyond the mind, body, ego, and senses. With your next inhale, reach your arms up and then release them down by your sides. Notice how you feel. Practice this flow one more time or as many times as you would like.

Seated Variation of Cactus Arms

You can practice this cactus arms variation in a chair or on the earth. If you are practicing this posture in a chair, take a seat and place your feet on the ground or onto blocks to bring the earth to you. Align your torso over your hips, and you can either allow the arms to extend down toward the earth or rest your hands on your knees, palms facing up or down. Relax your shoulders back and down, and reach up through the crown of your head. Take a few deep breaths here. If you are seated on the earth, you might choose to elevate your hips with a blanket or pillow. Rest your hands on your knees with the palms facing up or down. Allow your shoulders to relax back and down, and extend up through the crown of your head. Take a few deep breaths.

As you feel ready, inhale, sweeping your arms up overhead. As you sweep your arms out and up overhead, you might begin to feel your connection to that which is around you—the people, plants, air, elements, energies, etc. Once your arms are overhead, bend your elbows and make cactus arms. Your palms can face forward as you open your heart and draw your shoulder blades together. Take three deep breaths. Notice your front and back body. Notice the opening happening across your chest. Open to Spirit and feel the expansive nature of your own spirit. Open to what is available from the heart and beyond the mind, body, ego, and senses. With your next inhale, reach your arms up and then release them down by your sides. Notice how you feel. Practice this flow one more time or as many times as you would like.

PRANAYAMA

You can combine this pranayama practice with the meditation on page 90, or you can practice it as an individual practice.

Sama Vritti

For this practice, you will move through *sama vritti*, box breath or equal-part breathing. This pranayama practice is believed to quiet the mental chatter in the mind, which is often connected to our senses, thoughts, ego, worries, fears, and desires. This pranayama practice can support one in feeling less anxious due to the quieting nature it can have on the mind and the relaxing state it can create. It is from a restful and easeful state we are able to more clearly remember our true nature, realize who we are beyond our egos, desires, thoughts, and senses, and connect to the larger Self, Spirit, and all things.

You will equalize the length of your inhale and exhale.

Find a comfortable way to be in your body.

Place your hands on your knees with the palms facing up or down.

Close your eyes, or find a soft gaze on the ground in front of you.

Begin by taking a few deep breaths, feeling the breath fill the body and release from the body.

After you've taken a few deep breaths, begin to equalize the length of your inhales and exhales. Sometimes people do this by counting the breath. If counting works for you, great. If not, you can let go of the counting. Continue to equalize the length of your inhales and exhales for at least 2 minutes, perhaps a bit longer. After you have completed this pranayama practice, slow the breath in and out and take your time to come back into your space.

Take a moment to notice what consciousness you have gained from the practice. Notice if there is anything your Higher Self would like to communicate to you at this time.

MEDITATION

This meditation is focused on moving from a place of "I-amness" to "we-areness."

Find a comfortable way to be in your body—seated, lying down, or standing.

Once you have found your posture, and if you are seated, place your hands on your knees, your palms facing up or down. If you are standing, you might decide to place your arms by your side.

We-areness Meditation

Close your eyes, or find a soft gaze on the ground in front of you.

Take a few deep breaths to ground and center yourself.

Begin to breathe more deeply, offering a deeper inhale and a longer exhale. Feel the flow of breath as it moves into your body and out of your body.

After several deep breaths and the next time you inhale, I invite you to consider who you are beyond your ego, identities, desires, thoughts, and senses. Who are you beyond your human experience? Images or words may come into your awareness. Allow them to emerge without getting fixated on them. Who are you beyond your individual experience? Take a few deep breaths.

Now, I invite you to consider who you are in relation to the entire collective. Who are you when you remember you are an extension of the whole? Who are you when you move from an individual to who you truly are, which is part of the collective and pure consciousness?

Take a few deep breaths.

When you are ready to move out of this meditation, move out of it slowly. Gently come back into your space and take some time to reorient, hopefully feeling a deeper connection to your true Self.

MUDRA

You may be familiar with *Jnana* mudra. It is known as the sacred hand gesture meant to channel the vital life-force energy, prana. It is a mudra that supports practitioners in becoming less focused on the ego and works to destroy egoic tendencies that lead to separation and forgetting who we truly are. According to yoga philosophy, each finger on your hand corresponds to a planet, an emotion, an element, and a quality about your personality or karma. The index finger, which is part of Jnana mudra, represents Venus and Mars, fire and the ego, and the thumb, which is also part of Jnana mudra, represents Jupiter, air, and consciousness.

Jnana Mudra

Find a comfortable way to be in your body.

Take a few deep breaths to ground and center yourself.

Once you feel centered, tuck your index finger under the tip of your thumb to form a circle. All the other three fingers extended. Your hands can rest on your knees with the palms facing upward. A variation of this gesture is to touch the tip of the index finger and thumb together, thereby forming a full circle. To receive the maximum benefits from this practice, I suggest you sit in meditation while holding this mudra for 10 to 15 minutes. I recognize this may be a long time to sit, and I encourage you to begin with 2 to 5 minutes, working up to 10 to 15 minutes. You can practice this mudra as you move through the meditation listed above, or you can find a meditative state and practice this mudra coupled with pranayama, movement, or on its own. Jnana mudra is most commonly practiced in meditation.

MANTRA

OM NAMAH SHIVAYA

OM means the vibration that represents the creation of the universe

Namah means to bow or show adoration

Shivaya means the inner self

I have chanted and spoken this mantra for almost a decade. This mantra is dedicated to Lord Shiva, who is known as the deity associated with destruction and transformation. Om Namah Shivaya is one of the most powerful mantras in Hinduism. Repeating this mantra can lead you back to the Higher Self and support you in removing negative energies and transforming egoic patterns that are in the way of you remembering you are part of the universal consciousness. This mantra acknowledges and affirms that you are part of the collective and is a practice of bowing to your true inner self, accepting yourself as part of the collective universal consciousness.

Part Three

Raga and Our Attachments

This part offers an introduction to the third klesha—raga, or an attachment to pleasure. This section explores the difference between pleasure, joy, and peace. It explains what can happen when we enter a cycle of wanting to recreate a pleasurable experience, because the truth is, we can never recreate a moment in time again; each moment is new, and all that we experience in our lives is temporary. This section ends with practices focused on cultivating the skill of presence. The practices support the reader in being in the cosmic flow of life and working to be present to it all.

7

Raga

Attachment is that which dwells upon pleasure.

—Yoga Sutra 2.7, translated by Swami Prabhavananda
and Christopher Isherwood in *How to Know God:*
The Yoga Aphorisms of Patanjali

I HAD A BEAUTIFUL wedding in Greensboro, North Carolina, many years ago. My then-partner and I planned the ceremony and invited our friends to play a central role in it, from officiant to makeup artist to DJ. We found the perfect caterer and cake maker. On the first shopping trip I took with my mom to look for wedding dresses, I found an exquisite dress that didn't need any alterations. I made the wedding favors—leaf-shaped pottery spoon rests for the guests. My co-worker arranged the flowers and made ceremony decorations and centerpieces. We had a rehearsal dinner at a little Italian restaurant, and the day after, we got hitched on a rooftop. It rained during the ceremony, a sign of good luck, so they say. The sun came out after it rained, and it was as if a storm hadn't even passed through during the ceremony.

It was a beautiful ceremony and a joyous occasion. We had over 140 guests join us. We were elated to be surrounded by friends and family. So much preparation went into it, and the time spent during our wedding whizzed by. I can barely remember saying hello to guests or cutting a rug on the dance floor. What had taken months to plan culminated in a five-hour event. The morning after our wedding, we had brunch with some guests and headed back home to pack and prepare for a mountain getaway for our honeymoon.

The sadness about the ceremony and wedding party being over didn't set in until we were in our bed-and-breakfast in Asheville, North Carolina. I looked at Jeff over poached eggs and coffee and said, "I feel depressed our wedding is over." He looked at me, a little bit perplexed by my reaction. He wasn't feeling sad or depressed. I would imagine it is quite normal to feel sad when something so momentous and joyous, such as a wedding, is over. I would imagine it is quite normal to feel sad when friends and family leave after they have celebrated you, your love, and your union in such a profound way. Even so, there was something about the sadness I felt at that time that even stood out to me. To me, it felt as if the joy was so short-lived, and while I knew we could not relive our ceremony as it happened, I wanted the joy I felt leading up to and during the ceremony to remain.

The sadness I felt dissipated over time, and throughout the years, Jeff and I intentionally set aside time to remember our wedding ceremony. On anniversaries, we would look at pictures and remember the joyous time spent with friends and family. We celebrated our ten-year wedding anniversary with a big party, and many of the same guests, as well as new guests, joined us for the celebration. Had my sadness led me to form an unhealthy attachment to the memory of the wedding ceremony, so much so that I tried to recreate it in my mind or literally recreate it with the same caterer, flowers, friends, music, and sensations, this would have led to suffering for Jeff and me. The exact joy I felt on my wedding night was a joy I couldn't recreate. I could only create new memories but would never be able to recreate the exact conditions that led me to feel the way I did the first time I was married.

The third klesha is raga. It is the klesha that creates samskaras focused on an attachment to pleasure. It can create obstacles for us if our pleasant memories lead us to revisit the past in a way that is attached to wanting to recreate it versus remembering it. Because objects can be associated with pleasant memories, this can motivate one to acquire objects in an effort to recreate a memory or feeling. Raga can also lead one to become addicted to objects they perceive as or experience bringing pleasure to them. This can cause an unhealthy attachment to objects and an addiction to pleasure.

> Affliction that has pleasure as its resting ground is attachment.
> —YOGA SUTRA 2.7, TRANSLATED BY PANDIT RAJMANI TIGUNAIT IN
> *THE PRACTICE OF THE YOGA SUTRA: SADHANA PADA*

As I explore raga in this chapter, please know I am aware that we each may have received mixed messages about our desire to feel pleasure and joy. I understand, given our various social locations, we may have received cultural messages that suggest we are undeserving of pleasure. We will explore this in great detail in chapter 8. In this chapter, I will explain how raga might show up in your life and the patterns that may emerge if you become attached to pleasure, and how this attachment can lead you to experience suffering.

Sharing the example of my first wedding ceremony may seem like an extreme way to illustrate how raga can show up in our lives. While I caught myself and noticed my sadness after my first wedding ceremony was over, and even normalized the sadness I felt, and while in my marriage to Jeff I didn't actively try to recreate my wedding ceremony and the exact joy I felt when I got married or the pleasant feeling that came from celebrating love with friends and family, the example is also present for me because I recently remarried. Much like my first wedding, I planned the ceremony with my partner. We planned the menu, decorations, flowers, lights, the right-sized tent, farm tables and benches, programs, and beeswax candles as well as the special water from Shatley Springs, North Carolina, that we served our guests. We planned every detail because we are planners, but also because the ceremony was to take place in our backyard.

We had fifty guests join us for a ceremony full of rituals involving honeybees, hens, and blessings. I wore purple instead of white, and my partner wore the most fabulous pants strewn with gold, silver, and black. He adorned his shirt with a bee pendant, and we danced our way into the night and seasonal shift on the fall equinox in 2022. Of course, I wanted it to be a joyous occasion, and it was, but I didn't approach it in a way that led me to want to recreate the same exact ceremony I had with Jeff. Charles and I didn't choose the same caterer or cake maker, and we didn't create the same kind of ceremony. Sure, it took place in the fall because it is one of our favorite seasons, but we chose a different date and had a theme, A Taste of Honey. This was to honor not only the honeybees but also all the sweetness we were calling into our lives on that day and into the future. Mostly new friends for me and many long-time friends for Charles, as well as some of our family members, joined us. It was beautiful but not the same as my wedding ceremony with Jeff. It wasn't meant to be the same. Both were joyful ceremonies and times in my life, but not the same. Between the time of my first wedding to Jeff and my magical ceremony with Charles, there was joy and pain and whatever exists between joy and pain, because both joy and pain are fleeting, just as is every experience we have.

Our minds work in a way that makes us categorize things as pleasant or unpleasant. Often there isn't a gray space or in-between space. Many of us are conditioned to think in binaries, which includes how we relate to experiences. Often our mental patterns, as well as our perception of experience, teaches us to relate to things as pleasant or unpleasant. Sometimes we relate to different experiences we have as enjoyable or painful, not as enjoyable *and* painful. Raga causes us to cling to memories that make us feel pleasure, along with the objects associated with these memories, in an attempt to recreate these memories to feel full spiritually and emotionally. When objects we associate with pleasure aren't available, at times we can begin to feel empty or like life is out to get us or that something is wrong with us. In chapter 8, I share some about the system of capitalism, which conditions us to believe we aren't enough as we are and that we cannot find an abiding state of peace on our own but rather through a need for objects to make us whole and good enough. This conditioning also influences how empty people may feel and the tendency to become addicted to things that provide a temporary sense of pleasure or a false sense of pleasure.

Raga can lead one to begin to chase pleasure. This is where addictions are born. In my previous example of my weddings, of course, I didn't become addicted to wedding planning or insist on yearly ceremonies to celebrate anniversaries and to recreate my wedding ceremony experiences and bliss. I just noticed my response to something like a wedding ceremony—that by design, as with everything else in life, was always a fleeting and temporary experience. I noticed my sadness and explored why it was present, and paid attention to how my sadness connected to my desire for more time with family and friends. I also noticed if it was related to wanting to chase down that feeling of bliss and connection again. In planning my second wedding, I paid attention to whether or not I was trying to emulate anything from the first one.

There are certainly other ways raga shows up in my life. Perhaps in more subtle ways, subtler than a wedding ceremony. It has shown up through how I relate to food, substances like alcohol and chocolate, and shopping. It has shown up in my romantic relationships because of my desire to hold on to pleasant things, things that made me feel whole, or something other than pain. In these relationships, raga made me develop an unhealthy attachment to people and deny the toxicity that was present because of how these relationships, at times, were causing more harm than good. I have felt addicted to people or how people have made me feel. I have developed unhealthy attachments to good wine and dark chocolate. At one point in my life, I was spending more money than I had and buying unnecessary things. I always want to blame this on being a Leo sun because we can be indulgent, but it's deeper than my astrology. I would spend beyond my means to cover up pain or experience temporary moments of joy. I don't sit in a place of judgment about these things now. I offer these as other examples for you to begin to consider how raga is showing up in your life.

The more often we try to recreate an experience of pleasure, the stronger our attachment to it grows. We become confused because of our attachment to pleasure, be that from objects, people, or memories, and it becomes difficult to discern between ourselves and our desires. This confusion causes so much strife and pain. Though in my life I have developed an unhealthy attachment to things like wine, food, and relationships and, at times, felt temporary pleasure and joy from these things, I don't want to suggest that someone who is addicted to alcohol, drugs, sex, TV, chocolate, shopping, or another substance or material item feels pleasure as they are chasing their next fix. Or to suggest that when we are struggling with addiction, we aren't in pain. I understand addiction to substances, material things, and relationships is painful. I understand that becoming addicted to a way of thinking can be painful. I know addiction often arises from a painful place or experience.

Often, when I have struggled with any type of addiction—sought out a glass of wine, binge-watched trash television, or filled up my Amazon cart—it was because I wanted to escape something painful or because I wasn't paying attention to what I was doing, or both. These patterns derive from the way, at times, I and others can move through life without paying attention to what we are doing and how things can blur our ability to clearly see and fully notice the actions we choose to take. This is one of the ways raga intersects with avidya and asmita. We don't clearly see; we confuse our identities, egos, and desires with who we are, and we become addicted to things that bring only pleasure and resist that which we perceive as causing pain, and we avoid unpleasant things. It is a cycle. Pain could lead us to want only pleasure, but pleasure is fleeting, and the loss of it can cause pain. The experience of pleasure could cause us to seek out only pleasure as if pain and suffering aren't part of the human experience. This cycle—and in particular raga and dvesha, the next klesha we will explore in chapter 10—doesn't allow us to be in the present moment or the fullness of our human experience—the pleasure, joy, pain, beauty, suffering, and places of respite where we are not feeling pain or pleasure.

I believe, during both of my wedding ceremonies, I was in the present moment. During my first wedding ceremony, I remember my father stepping all over my wedding dress. He was beginning to go blind and couldn't really see where his size 12 feet were stepping. I remember how people spoke blessings into the ether for us as the sky opened and rain poured down. I remember the sunflowers and how vibrant they were. I remember my friends dancing to the Beastie Boys on the makeshift dance floor. I remember how free I felt while I was dancing. I remember my friend Kelly reading a Rainer Rilke poem about love.

During my second wedding ceremony, I remember walking outside onto my deck and down the steps with Charles through our yard where dahlias and the butterfly bush were waiting to receive us. I remember listening to my dear friends Katie and Dani chanting and inviting the crowd to join in. I can still smell the propolis smudge wafting through the air. I remember washing Charles's hands and him washing mine with river water from the second oldest river in the world and water from the so-called fountain of youth. I was present to it all.

When sadness set in that my first wedding was over, I was no longer present to the honeymoon, fall colors, waterfalls we went to visit, taste of the poached eggs we were eating, or my then-partner, Jeff. I was present to what I was missing—a pleasant experience that, all of a sudden, I was missing. With my most recent ceremony, had I tried to chase pleasure and recreate the same ceremony I had with Jeff, I would have missed out on all of the beautiful memories of that night mentioned above. Raga takes us away from the present moment because it causes us to chase something that can never again be. It takes us away from what we are experiencing in the here and now. It can cause the mind to wander in ways that aren't in service of being fully alive and present to what is unfolding in real time, right now.

Raga, like all of the other kleshas, creates obstacles to our liberation and ability to feel unencumbered by the mind and the way it can move us into dead-end spaces that aren't good for us or anyone else. It pulls us away from the truth of who we are, the present moment, and at times, our purpose. Raga can move us away from ourselves and our communities. It can cause us to take actions that aren't in service of our higher selves or the collective. We are all subject to experiencing raga. The question is not *if* raga is showing up in your life; the question is *how* it is showing up in your life. In the next chapter, I offer a nuanced look at raga, given the confusing cultural messages many of us may have received about pleasure and joy. I add complexities to the content offered throughout this chapter about raga focused on our relationship with pleasure.

REFLECTION QUESTIONS

For now, please reflect on the following questions. As you reflect, remember previous practices offered in *Illuminating Our True Nature*. They may support you in being gentle and extending compassion to yourself as you reflect on how raga has shown up in the past and is showing up in your life now.

▶ How have you noticed raga showing up in your life in the past?

▶ How is it presently showing up for you?

▶ What patterns of indulgence, addiction, or attachment to objects, memories, or relationships have you noticed in yourself?

▶ What memories and objects do you find yourself returning to in your mind or the material realm?

▶ How might an attachment to experiencing only pleasure cause suffering or present obstacles in your life?

8

Healing Our Relationship to Pleasure

There is no way to repress pleasure and expect
liberation, satisfaction, or joy.
—ADRIENNE MAREE BROWN, *PLEASURE ACTIVISM:
THE POLITICS OF FEELING GOOD*

IT WAS FRIDAY evening. We were preparing to cozy up to the television. The gas fireplace emitted warmth and flames and created a nice aesthetic. To ensure optimal coziness, I gathered up the quilt my great-grandmother had made for us. My mom was grabbing the Cheez-Its from the kitchen. I sat on the couch, and my mom, Cheez-Its in hand, sat in her recliner. At 9 P.M., *Dynasty* would come on, followed by *Falcon Crest*, and we were in place with our late-night snacks. I remember the salty, cheesy smell when my mother would open the box; my mouth watered in anticipation of the crunch of the first Cheez-It. By 11 P.M., and once the closing music to *Falcon Crest* was playing, my mom and I would have made fast work of the Cheez-Its. The box would be empty, without a crumb in sight. This experience of Cheez-Its, my beloved mother, and night soaps brought me so much joy when I was a child. Some would say it was our guilty pleasure, but for me it was a time to connect with my mom—a ritual of sorts.

Over time, this ritual stopped because I became a teenager and started to spend Friday nights at the mall or movie theater with my friends. I also became more self-conscious about my body size and shape. I stopped eating things I perceived as junk food, started eating salads, and ultimately restricted my food options throughout the end of high school and into college. During this time, it seemed as if food wasn't meant to be enjoyed; more often, I saw it as an enemy. Diet culture and dominant cultural norms about body shape and size and what foods were considered to be healthy reinforced the idea that starving oneself to be thin was the pathway to wellness. These norms took the enjoyment out of food and rituals focused on food, like breaking bread with others or eating a box of Cheez-Its with my mom.

> Recollection or memory (*smriti*) is mental modification caused by the inner reproducing of a previous impression of an object, but without adding any other characteristics from other sources.
> —YOGA SUTRA 1.11, TRANSLATED BY SWAMI JNANESHVARA IN "TRADITIONAL YOGA AND MEDITATION OF THE HIMALAYAN MASTERS"[9]

Until very recently, I had forgotten all about Cheez-Its, *Dynasty, Falcon Crest,* and cozy Friday evenings with my mom. About a month ago, my partner's daughter, Ana, came home with a box of Cheez-Its. When I saw the box, I felt happy but didn't know why at the time. I also felt some sense of dread because I knew I wouldn't be able to stop myself from eating the Cheez-Its once the box was open. This tasty snack of cheesy goodness wasn't meant for me. It was on Ana's shelf in the pantry and was meant to enhance her school lunch. Yoga Sutra 1.11 speaks to how memories are formed through previous impressions or experiences with objects. This is what happened for me when I saw the box of Cheez-Its, although I didn't recognize it until a few weeks later. When she went to school on Wednesday and to her mom's house for the rest of the week and weekend, Ana left a half-full Cheez-Its box, and I couldn't resist. As I ate them, they tasted so good. The cheesy crunch made it very difficult for me to stop eating them. This became a pattern. Ana would leave opened boxes of Cheez-Its on her shelf in the pantry, and week after week, I would finish them.

I started to feel bad about eating them. During a recent walk with a friend, we were talking about the kleshas and raga. I was thinking about mindlessly eating Cheez-Its while recognizing there are other examples of raga that may be much more harmful than Cheez-Its. I said to my friend, "I know I don't want to eat them. Often, I reach for them late at night when I am tired and/or bored and want to crunch on something." Upon sharing this with my friend, I remembered the childhood memory of spending time with my mom, watching our night soap operas and dramas, and making a tasty snack out of something as simple as Cheez-Its. I realized the food was connected to a memory of spending time with my mom. As I made this realization, my heart felt warmed by a wonderful childhood ritual we shared together. While I am trying to figure out my relationship with Cheez-Its, and ultimately practice discernment and notice when I am reaching for something outside of myself to feel pleasure or joy, I am also trying to figure out the mixed messages I received about pleasure. I am trying to disentangle judgments about the food I choose to eat. I am working to allow myself to indulge in what some might call guilty pleasures. I am working to shed any toxic messaging I have received about my being worthy of experiencing joy and pleasure. While Cheez-Its may seem to provide a simple example of becoming attached to something, clearly they aren't that simple. Everything is layered.

Chapter 7 introduced the third klesha, raga, and explored how raga, or an attachment to pleasure, can lead to suffering. This chapter adds nuance and texture to the concepts explored in chapter 7. This chapter delves into how our socialization and shaping inform our relationship with pleasure. In this chapter, at times, I use the words *pleasure* and *joy* synonymously. They are not exactly the same thing, but they are deeply related to one another. Pleasure is often thought of as a mental state and joy as an emotion. The stories and framing I have chosen to use in this chapter highlight for me how pleasure is connected to joy and our desire to feel joyful.

We are in deep relationship with ourselves; we can, in fact, create pleasurable experiences for ourselves, just as we encounter outside sources that might bring us joy. We can also feel joy in response to a pleasurable experience we created, just as we can feel joy in response to something pleasurable that occurs because of an interaction with someone or something outside of ourselves. As you read this chapter, I invite you to consider how joy and pleasure intersect for you and your understanding of these two parts of the human experience. As you read, please know that, as I consider my relationship to pleasure and reflect on the stories shared with me by the myriad people I come into contact with, so many of us are working to identify and disentangle ourselves from the mixed-up messages we may have received about pleasure and our right to experience it. This chapter works to support us in the disentangling process while continuing to look at where our relationship with pleasure may be out of balance.

While it felt joyful to be in a bubble with a box of Cheez-Its and watch late-night television with my mother, I don't remember us describing the experience as pleasurable. I remember us just being in the experience. In fact, I don't remember receiving many messages about pleasure from my mother or other family members. Mostly, we didn't talk about pleasure. It wasn't that we couldn't enjoy things, but pleasure wasn't the frame we used to describe things that brought us joy.

I don't remember learning about pleasure or joy while I attended school. I remember rules meant to keep us in line and assimilate us into a system that may not have cared much about our pleasure, joy, or if we were suffering. Even so, I do remember moments of joy, in particular while playing hopscotch on the playground or playing with an uninflated hot-air balloon as children held onto its edges and made a fan out of it. We would scurry underneath it from one side to the next, laughing the entire time.

In some faith communities, people are shamed or persecuted for overindulging or feeling joy. This wasn't my experience in my faith community, although I imagine if someone at church felt as if I had lost my way, they would have judged me for not being reverent or living into the vision God held for me. In large part, the focus at church was getting to the kingdom of heaven, where we would be free of our bodies and sins and accepted with open arms and in all our glory. The joy I felt in church came from listening to the vibration that resonated as the choir sang. Joy and pleasure came from watching people be moved by God in a way that felt like they were free and liberated souls.

While I had pleasurable and joyful experiences at home, school, and church, and didn't receive many negative messages about my right to feel pleasure in these spaces, I did receive messages from dominant culture about pleasure. I received messages about who was entitled to experience it and who was not. I learned over time that as a Black person in a cisgender female body, my pleasure wasn't to be centered. I learned this from the way white supremacy culture assumed I was subhuman and therefore didn't deserve to feel pleasure or joy. I learned that having a female body in a patriarchal society meant that my pleasure wasn't as important as my responsibility to pleasure someone who has been socialized as a male. I learned, based on gender and race, that my needs weren't as important as people who embody identities that place them in closer proximity to social and institutional power.

As I moved through the world, I was confronted by dominant cultural norms rooted in control and supremacy. Dominant culture normalized the objectification of the bodies of those less proximal to power. People and systems appropriated spiritual practices such as yoga and cultural practices related to dress, customs, and the celebration of certain holidays like the Dios de la Muerte. I experienced the system of capitalism trying to sell objects and experiences to me under the guise of these objects and experiences bringing me joy or pleasure. Sometimes what I was being sold was only meant to bring temporary pleasure. Sometimes what I was being sold or asked to consume from the capitalist culture was a sense of false pleasure. And often, what I was being sold or asked to consume by way of capitalism and other systems of dominance was predicated on the fact that something was wrong with me and needed to be fixed, that I wasn't enough as I am and needed something to make me a better person. This all feels like a twisted orientation to pleasure and our enoughness.

I worked in countless nonprofit organizations where pleasure and joy weren't centered as we did our work. The often unspoken intention was to work ourselves to death for whatever cause we were fighting for and to put aside our desire for pleasure and joy in our lives and work. The institutionalization of a practice of decentering one's pleasure or right to feel joy as they do their work is dangerous because it limits our ability to express the fullness of who we are and creates obstacles to fully living into our humanity as free and liberated souls.

As I navigated the world, I learned that some people's comfort, pleasure, and needs are centered while others are negated. The core messages I have received from dominant culture about pleasure and joy support the idea that there is a hierarchy related to who is deserving of pleasure. The constructed identities we embody often shape narratives about whether or not we are deserving of pleasure. Some of us are told it is okay to feel pleasure and create pleasurable experiences for ourselves and others. Some of us are taught to shut down the part of us that may want to feel pleasure. Herein lies why, at times, I feel confused about pleasure and joy and their place in my life.

The experience of being in a human body with different identities, and the awareness of how these identities have shaped me and influenced my relationship to pleasure and joy, coupled with being a spiritual being and practitioner, have placed me in a space of review and reflection about the messages I have internalized about pleasure. My human and spiritual paths have led me to be curious about and, at times, interrogate the messages I have internalized about pleasure, dispelling messages that aren't useful or helpful about my and others' right to experience pleasure. This practice of reflection and review derives from a place of wanting to have a healthy and intentional relationship with pleasure and to work to notice when I am overly attached to something or have developed what I would consider to be an unhealthy attachment to something.

The path of yoga has taught me that I can find a state of peace inside and return to this state time and time again. I can find joy from the inside out. I can also find joy and experience pleasure through connection with others. The path of yoga also reminds me that joy and pleasure come from an awareness of my interconnectedness to all things, which then propels me to be of service to something bigger than myself and practice selflessness. While I have wrangled around in my head about Cheez-Its and other indulgences, what I can say now is that what felt so pleasurable and joyful about spending time with my mom on Friday evenings was that we were connecting with one another. The food was attached to the memory of a very meaningful connection. I liken this meaningful connection to other things outside of myself that bring pleasure because they remind me of my connection to all things and remind me I am alive—things like the sound of a child laughing, my mother's smile, a very nice glass of wine, John Coltrane, and a warm fire.

Raga exists because of a misunderstanding that pleasure, like everything, is temporary. It is a misunderstanding about or confusion of actual needs and desires. At this time, in our collective, on a mass scale, raga is creating an imbalance and social unrest. It is important for us to remember this and work to shift the obstacles it creates in our lives and the collective. It is also important to understand the cultural context and conflicting and confusing messages we receive about pleasure and attachment. While we strive to break patterns that lead to suffering, we must also look at the flawed messages dominant culture gives us about why we suffer. Dominance isn't rooted in spiritual practice or liberation. It is rooted in separation, an attachment to power, and misperception about the true Self. My desire to feel pleasure or engage in activities that might bring me joy is, at times, in direct response to the ways I have been told not to feel pleasure. My desire to feel pleasure and claim joy as my birthright derives from my practice of seeking to gain clarity and clear sight about who I truly am. My desire to feel pleasure and to experience joy take root amid a culture that professes and operates as if there is a hierarchy of bodies, only prioritizes the right to comfort for those more proximal to power, and shames people for wanting to feel pleasure.

REFLECTION QUESTIONS

Thus far, in this chapter, I have shared some of the messages I have received about pleasure based on my identities, dominant culture, and narratives about pleasure. I want to provide an opportunity for you to reflect on the messages you have received about pleasure. The questions that follow may stir up emotions and memories. To begin with, you might decide to answer one question and sit with your response, giving yourself space and time between reflection questions. Be gentle with yourself as you explore these questions.

- ▶ What messages did you receive from family and community about pleasure and your right to experience it?
- ▶ What messages did you receive about joy as your birthright?
- ▶ What messages did you receive from institutions such as the

educational system, healthcare system, housing, labor, etc., about pleasure?

▶ What messages did you receive from dominant culture about pleasure? Were you entitled to it, or was your pleasure decentered?

▶ What did you learn about different groups of people and their right to experience pleasure and joy?

We Deserve

Given the fact that so many of us have received conflicting messages about our right to pleasure and our experience and expression of joy, it feels important to name this: in our human bodies, we deserve to feel pleasure and joy. We will undoubtedly experience sorrow, loss, and dissonance because these are things we will experience as humans. Given this, it is important to acknowledge that we can, will, and should also feel and experience pleasure and joy. What else feels important to share is that, if I prioritize my joy and pleasure over someone else's liberation and access to pleasure and joy, then I am not operating out of the Higher Self or from a place of clearly seeing my connection to all things.

To me, the question isn't whether or not it was okay to eat Cheez-Its with my mom and watch television and gossip about the characters on *Dynasty* and *Falcon Crest*. The question is, was that experience of pleasure and joy harming others? Was I attached to the experience in a way that caused harm to myself or others? Was I engaging in it at the expense of others? Did it become a pattern that was causing harm to myself? Was I engaging mindlessly in the pattern? These feel like the questions we need to ask ourselves instead of whether or not we are deserving of pleasure and joy.

The mixed messages we may have received about pleasure and joy, and the messages that have shaped our relationship to pleasure and joy, could cause us to never allow ourselves to engage in pleasurable activities or to fully feel joy. The task through practice is to allow these experiences of pleasure to occur without becoming overly attached to them, to notice when we have become attached, and to counter any false messages that influence our ability to allow pleasure and joy to have a space in our lives. If we crave pleasure in a world that asks so many of us not to crave what it is we desire and works to dampen our aliveness, may we forgive ourselves? May we practice in an effort to better understand the root of our cravings, the cost of our cravings, and contemplate the liberation that might come from disrupting the idea that so many of us aren't seen as deserving of pleasure?

Healing Our Relationship to Pleasure

What has been revealed to me through my spiritual practice is that its intention is to bring me back to wholeness. Part of the process of returning to wholeness requires me to heal any fractures caused by my shaping and conditioning around my relationship to pleasure and joy. I could choose to be at odds with myself and the box of Cheez-Its that sits atop a shelf in the pantry now, or I could choose to feel the full taste of a Cheez-It and not beat myself up for even contemplating eating it. Sitting with my mother in her living room was part of coming into wholeness in a world that didn't want us—me in my child Black body and my mom in her adult Black body—to feel joy, laughing and carrying on late into the night.

To conclude this chapter, I offer a practice for cultivating a healthy relationship with pleasure and joy. My hope is that you come to peace with yourself and that you come to know it's okay—better than okay—to feel pleasure. Healing our relationship with pleasure and joy and illuminating all that is in the way of us feeling fully alive is what spiritual practice offers.

CULTIVATING A HEALTHY RELATIONSHIP WITH PLEASURE PRACTICE

Take a moment to find a way to be in your body—seated, on your back, standing, still, or in motion. Take a few deep breaths, inviting in ease and calm. Take a moment to bring something or someone into your awareness that brings pleasure to you. If you are focusing on something that brings pleasure to you, you might think about a landscape, piece of art, song, special crystal, or sacred object. If you are focusing on someone who brings pleasure to you, you might think about specific actions this person takes in their life that inspire you, words they may have shared with you, experiences you have shared with them, or future experiences you've planned with them. You might think about them being who they are and how their way of being brings pleasure to you. Take a moment to breathe and to be with the sensation of pleasure. Notice how you feel in your body and heart as you do.

Continue to breathe and repeat the following mantra:

I desire a healthy relationship with that which brings pleasure to me.

Repeat this mantra three times.

Take three deep breaths after the mantra has been spoken three times.

Come back into your space, and write down any reflections or new insights from this short activity.

9

Presence

Cut the cords of attachment. Expand the circle of love.

—SHRI RADHE MAA

I N *Illuminating Our True Nature*, much of what has been explored about raga thus far has focused on attachment to pleasurable or pleasant experiences, memories, or objects. This chapter explores the absolute truth that everything is temporary: both pleasurable and unpleasant experiences, memories, and objects. Every experience, emotion, and human experience is temporary. I have shared many examples of raga related to food, substances, and relationships. In this chapter, I share about my mother—I share a story about a moment when we believed she was close to death and the process of transitioning out of her physical body and the ethereal realm, and I share about a teaching this experience offered me. I share about my mother because my experiences with her—both how I came into the world, my birth story, and how she almost left the world—feel like the most potent teachers I've had about the temporary nature of things. Raga, an attachment to pleasure, and dvesha, an attachment to aversion—which is the next klesha we will explore, in chapter 10—create obstacles in our lives because our minds want to resist the temporary nature of everything. This chapter and practices remind us of what it is to experience and notice pleasant times, to expect there to be times or experiences we move through that are unpleasant, and to meet the moment as it is, whatever our experience might be.

In 2019 and 2020, my mother, Clara, became very ill. She was hospitalized twice, in and out of skilled nursing facilities, and on the brink of death. One day, the hospital doctors told me there wasn't anything further they could do. They had planned to transfer my mother to a skilled nursing facility. Given the physical and mental state she was in at the time, a transfer seemed unreasonable to me, but I assumed they needed to free up the hospital bed. My mother had stopped eating and was barely drinking anything; medicine was being pumped into her system nonstop. She had fleeting moments of lucidity and many moments of confusion. She did not seem like herself.

When the doctors shared there wasn't anything else they could do, this signaled to me that we might transfer my mother to a skilled nursing facility only for her to die there. As this awareness began to sink into my consciousness and heart, I sat with my mom while she lay in her hospital bed. And while I sat with her, two very profound things happened. First, my mother asked me about my father. She said, "I guess we need to call your father." I was unsure what to say, because my father had been dead for more than three years. I responded, "Dad isn't alive anymore. He passed away. Do you remember?" Even though I felt the best thing was to be honest, my directness may have felt abrupt to her. My mother's face became confused, and tears welled in her eyes. I felt emotionally gutted. Telling my mother information about my father that she once knew, and in particular, the news that he wasn't alive anymore, was excruciating.

Shortly after, my mother saw the rose quartz ring on my index finger. She touched it, and I asked her if she wanted to hold it. She nodded in affirmation. I handed her my rose quartz ring; she held and caressed it, tracing the stone with her fingers. I smiled and thought about the synchronicity of a stone connected to the heart and all that was happening to our hearts at the time. My mother may not have been aware she was working with my heart then, but when she handed the ring back to me and I placed it on my finger, it felt different. It felt as if it had been infused with some peace from the ancestors my mother had told me she was speaking with, along with the promise of my mother being free of physical pain—pain she had been living with for decades. Then, we sat in silence for a while. In these moments of suffering and connection, I felt so many emotions.

I felt heartbroken that my mother was sick and potentially dying. I felt so glad I was with her. It felt sweet to connect over rose quartz. It felt difficult to accept that my mother might die. I felt grateful I could spend time with her. These emotions and experiences all happened at the same time. Some felt very unpleasant and difficult, and others felt sweet and familiar. I say familiar because I know that, in my ancestral line, people sat with each other when they were preparing to transition. I know people sat with each other as they were giving birth. I know my people sat in circle and in community time and time again, celebrating and grieving. This is precisely what I was doing with my mother: I was witnessing her exactly as she was in that moment. I was trying to soak it all in, both the challenging parts of it and the sweet and tender parts. Had I not been present to my mother's and my own suffering and pain at the time, and to feeling the moments of connection and resonance, I wouldn't have been able to move into a space of acceptance about exactly what was happening. My mother was dying. Or so we thought. Everything dies. Everything is temporary.

Raga and dvesha cause suffering for us because these kleshas, and the samskaras that form in response to them, challenge the absolute truth that everything is temporary. As shared in chapter 2, Yoga Sutra 2.5 speaks to the pattern of suffering that emerges from our confusing the permanent with the impermanent. We get stuck in a cycle of attachment to pleasure or form an aversion to that which we do not like, and these behavior patterns disrupt our ability to be in the moment and accept all it presents to us at the time. What was so poignant about my experience with my mother was that, at a certain point, amid pain and rose quartz, I could just be with her and the moment as it was. I know spiritual practice equipped me to sit with her and be with her during what felt like her final stages of life in this incarnation of herself.

The path of yoga teaches us how to ride the waves of emotion, sensation, and experience through practices meant to bring us back into the present moment and to accept what is happening versus what happened in the past or what we anticipate happening in the future. The path of yoga reminds us that we aren't our emotions, sensations, or the thing we experience; instead, we are pure consciousness. As I sat with my mother, and she sat with me, allowing me to witness her in one of her most vulnerable states, I believe we both understood and even felt what it is like to remember that we are pure consciousness. My mother was completely dependent on others for her care. She was talking to the ancestors in anticipation of her transition. She was trying to make sense of it all. And I was practicing being with her. Just being. Not doing or fixing. Not changing. Accepting.

In this life, we will experience it all, and while I hope we enjoy our lives and live fully into who we are, I also wish for us to not be burdened by an attachment to pleasurable things we cannot recreate. I wish for us to not be burdened by an attachment to things we feel an aversion to and instead for us to be at peace with what is happening in each present moment. At the time of my writing this chapter, my mother is still alive. She has not yet transitioned. My experience of being with her during times when she was ill certainly make me appreciate the time I get to spend with her now. Whether we're watching television in her apartment in the retirement community or in some tiff about something we might not agree about, I appreciate it all, the sweetness and the challenges; the pleasant and the unpleasant.

I appreciate all of the experiences I am lucky enough to have with my mom because we recognize our inherent divinity and how we are linked by our divinity. Without my mother, I would not be here. It is also true now that, without me, my mother probably would have transitioned while lying in a bed in a skilled nursing facility in 2020. The interconnectedness of it all feels beautiful, and I want to strive to be present with my mother and present to all life has to offer me. We will continue to explore the theme of presence in the face of distraction, which moves us away from liberation, as we move on to the next chapter and klesha.

REFLECTION QUESTIONS

For now, I offer the following reflection questions and practices in the hopes they will support you in healing the wounds and suffering created by raga.

▶ What emotions arise when you recognize the temporary nature of all things?

▶ What or who allows you to come into the full presence of your life?

▶ What practices support you in coming into the present moment?

Asana

The asana portion of this section will focus on moving from one posture to the next while noticing the ending of one posture, the transition between postures, and the beginning of a new posture. You might decide you want to practice the two postures presented in chapters 3 and 6—Tadasana, or mountain pose, and cactus arms—as a warm-up to this flow. You could also choose to move through any kind of flow or asanas prior to exploring the flow described here. Please begin in Balasana, child's pose.

Balasana, Child's Pose

You can practice this seated in a chair, on a mat on the floor, or on your back. I will describe how to move into this on a mat first and then share other variations. Begin by moving into tabletop position. Come down to hands and knees and place your shoulders over your wrists and your hips over your knees. Your toes can be untucked if this is comfortable for you. To move into Balasana, you might choose to bring your knees wide or bring them close together. Take a deep breath in and press your seat toward your heels. Sometimes it can be helpful to place a bolster between your knees for a more restorative version of Balasana or to bring a bolster or pillow between the back of your legs and your calves. Your arms can be stretched out in front of you or down by your side. Take a few deep breaths in the posture.

If you would like to move into this in a chair, you can sit in a chair with your feet on the earth or with support underneath them to bring the earth to you. Find a tall spine, take a deep breath in, and round forward as you move your shoulders onto your back.

You could also choose to explore this on your back. If you choose this variation, move onto your back and stretch out. Then gently hug your knees to your chest. Take a few deep breaths.

After finding your variation of Balasana, and taking a few deep breaths, prepare to begin to flow. You could also choose to stay in the posture, breathing in and out while noticing the inhale, pause, exhale, and release. If you are in the first variation of Balasana described above, please take an inhale and rise back into tabletop. From here, begin to move through what is called cat and cow. With

 an inhale, allow your belly to drop, your heart to open, and your tailbone to lift. With an exhale, allow your spine to round and your chin to move in toward your chest. Flow for a few rounds of breath and allow the inhale to initiate the

heart opening, belly dropping, and tailbone lifting up toward the sky. Allow the exhale to initiate the spine rounding and the chin moving toward the chest.

Begin to notice the shape change in your body as you breathe in and out. Begin to notice the flow and the pause between postures. Begin to notice the beginning of one posture and the transition between cat and cow. Flow here for as long as you would like, working with the temporary nature of each asana and posture we flow through. Continue to move here with your breath, remembering the temporary nature of each cycle of breath. This flow is a reminder that everything is temporary, flowing, and moving. We move from moments of stillness into motion and from motion into stillness. We pause at times. This flow will support you in feeling what it is like to flow versus attaching to one way of being or doing. Move through at least five rounds of movement. Once this feels complete, press back into Balasana.

Seated Variation of Child's Pose

If you are in the seated variation of the posture, with an inhale, place your hands on your knees or a chair. Take a deep breath out. Then, with an inhale, open your heart and draw your shoulder blades in toward your spine. With an exhale, round your spine. Flow  in this way through seated cat and cow. Move in the same way I suggest above, allowing each breath to initiate the movement in

the body. Begin to notice the flow and the pause between postures. Begin to notice the beginning of one posture and the transition

between cat and cow. As with the other variations, stay here for as long as you would like. Move through at least five rounds of movement. Return to Balasana for a few rounds of breath.

Child's Pose Variation on Your Back

If you are on your back in Balasana, with an inhale, stretch your arms overhead and stretch out through your legs, a full-body stretch. With an exhale, round in, gently bringing your knees in to your chest. Repeat this several times at your own pace. Begin to notice the flow and the pause between postures. Begin to notice the beginning of one posture and the transition between postures. Flow here for as long as you would like, working with the temporary nature of each asana and posture we flow through. Flow here with your breath, remembering the temporary nature of each cycle of breath. This flow is a reminder that everything is temporary, flowing, and moving. We move from moments of stillness into motion and from motion into stillness. We pause at times. This flow will support you in feeling what it is like to flow versus attaching to one way of being or doing. Once this flow feels complete, return to Balasana for a few breaths.

Pranayama ——————————————————————

You can combine this pranayama practice with the meditation that follows, or you can practice it as an individual, separate practice.

Dirga Breath

For this practice, you will move through *Dirga pranayam*, which is a grounding, calming breath. I offer it here as a way of working with raga and non-attachment, because when I practice it, I take intentional pauses throughout the inhale and exhale and at the bottom and top of each breath cycle. I feel it is helpful because it is a calming and cooling breath and emulates what it feels like to expand and release, as most pranayama practices do. Since this chapter focuses on the temporary nature of things, it seems like an appropriate place for Dirga pranayam. Dirga is also the deity associated with maternal energy, and since I've invoked my mother's energy in this chapter, it only seems appropriate to practice Dirga pranayam. You can explore Dirga pranayam seated on the earth, in a chair, or on your back.

Once you've found your posture, take a few deep natural breaths. Dirga breath is the practice of allowing your lungs to fill a third of the way, and then pause. You'll then fill your lungs another third of the way, and pause. Finally, you'll fill your lungs all the way up to the top, and then pause, finding the top of the inhalation. You'll then empty and exhale in this same manner—releasing a third of the breath, another third, and the final third to reach the bottom of your exhale. Now, with your next inhale, fill your belly up with air and pause. Next, inhale into your rib cage and pause, then all the way to the top of your collarbone and pause. Exhale, emptying the air from your collarbone area, then pause. Next, empty a little more air from your ribs and feel your rib cage contract, and pause. Now empty all of the breath; the air will empty, and your belly will hug into center. On the next inhale, fill your belly up with air. When your belly is full, draw in a little more breath and let that air expand into your rib cage, causing the ribs to widen apart. Continue this practice for 10 breaths. After you've completed the practice, take a moment to return to a natural, fluid breath and notice how you feel.

MEDITATION

This meditation is focused on the temporary nature of things.

The Nature of Things Meditation

Find a comfortable way to be in your body—seated, lying down, or standing.

Once you have found your posture, if you are seated, place your hands on your knees, the palms facing up or down. If you are standing, you might decide to place your arms by your side.

Close your eyes, or find a soft gaze on the ground in front of you.

Take a few deep breaths to ground and center yourself.

Begin to breathe more deeply, exploring a deeper inhale and a longer exhale. Feel the flow of breath as it moves into your body and out of your body.

After several deep breath cycles, on an inhalation, guide your awareness to something that brings pleasure to you or to a pleasant experience. I invite you to notice all you can about it. Take a few deep breaths while you notice. Then open one of your hands and imagine you are holding that pleasant experience or object in your hand. Take a few deep breaths. Close your hand and make a fist with it. Breathe in and breathe out. Then open your hand, releasing the pleasurable object or experience. This isn't about

pretending it didn't happen; this is about allowing it to release and bringing your awareness back to your breath. You can practice this a few more times, working with the energy of bringing your awareness to a pleasant object or an experience that brought you joy. You'll imagine placing it in your hand, then making a fist, and then breathing and letting it go. After you've practiced this a few times, you can guide your awareness back to the breath, and as you feel ready, move out of the meditation.

Mudra

You may be familiar with *Gyan Vairagya* mudra. It represents the gesture of detachment. This mudra will feel similar to Jnana mudra. The difference here is the hands will be on the thighs rather than the kneecaps.

Gyan Vairagya Mudra

Find a comfortable way to be in your body.

Take a few deep breaths to ground and center yourself.

Once you feel centered, tuck your index finger under the tip of your thumb to form a circle. The other three fingers are extended. Your hands can rest on your thighs with the palms facing upward. A variation of this gesture is to touch the tip of the index finger and thumb together, thereby forming a full circle. To receive the maximum benefits from this practice, I suggest you sit in meditation while holding this mudra for 10 to 15 minutes. I recognize this may be a long time to sit. I encourage you to begin with 2 to 5 minutes, working slowly toward 10 to 15 minutes.

MANTRA

OM GAM GANAPATEYI NAMAHA

My salutations to Lord Ganesha.

OM: the vibration that represents the creation of the universe
GAM: the seed mantra for Ganesha
Ganapateyi: an alternate name for Ganesha

Ganesha is considered the deity associated with removing obstacles and bringing prosperity. As you chant this mantra, I invite you to invoke the power of Ganesha to support you in removing anything in the way of you being a free, liberated soul. I invite you to remember your divine spark and consciousness and to remove the pattern of becoming overly attached to pleasure, pain, or suffering.

As with Om Namah Shivaya, I have chanted and spoken this mantra for almost a decade. I have practiced it in *Japa* meditation and repeated this mantra 108 times as part of my morning practice. It is also the mantra I found myself chanting as I traversed my mother's illness. I didn't want anything to be in the way of her staying in this plane or moving to the heavenly plane. I invite you to say it at least 10 times, maybe working up to 108 times. Record any observations in your journal.

Part Four

Dvesha and Our Aversions

Part Four explores the fourth klesha—dvesha, or aversion to or avoidance of that which we believe we dislike. This klesha arises from the preceding ones, leading us to a place of wanting to potentially annihilate that which we do not believe we like or that which we believe we are averse to. This section explores how this klesha can show up for an individual and how it is showing up for us on a collective level. Part Four ends with practices intended to cultivate a more compassionate heart and way of being as well as practices that allow us to move back into a harmonious and balanced state of being.

10

Dvesha

I feel sorry for anybody that could let hate wrap them up. Ain't no
such thing as I can hate anybody and hope to see God's face.
—FANNIE LOU HAMER[10]

I N PREVIOUS SECTIONS, the kleshas have been explored through
stories about various topics. In this section, the way I explore dvesha, the next klesha, is through a story of racism enacted upon me
when I was a child. As explored in chapter 5, our social location and
identities inform how we will and do experience different things. I invite
BIPOC to take care of yourselves as you read this chapter. The content
contained in it might feel triggering or disrupt your nervous system. For
white-bodied folks, I invite you to stay with the material presented in this
chapter. The skill of staying with the truth presented is one thing that
can allow those more proximal to power to transform and change the
conditions in place that are in the way of us all being free.

I was in second grade. We were outside for recess, and I was playing
on the playground with my best friend, Alison. While we were playing
on the monkey bars, one of our peers—a white boy—walked across the
playground and approached us, spat at me, and called me a "nigger." I
was unfamiliar with the word. I hadn't ever heard it before, but I could
tell it wasn't positive, because the word was not only accompanied by spit
but also a scowl on the child's face as he said it to me. My friend, Alison,
told the child who disrupted our playtime to stop, and she called over

the teacher. I don't know what happened in the immediate moments that followed. I don't know what the teacher said, if anything. I don't know if we continued to play. I don't even remember how I was feeling. I just knew I had been called a name that spoke to how different I was from everyone else on the playground and in my class.

At that time, I was the only Black girl in my class. I had some friends, but in large part, I stuck out like a sore thumb. Even though I knew I was different, I didn't always have the language to describe what it felt like to be different. On the playground with Alison, I wasn't really aware of my difference. We were just two young girls playing on the monkey bars. The white boy who called me a "nigger" didn't allow us to be just two girls playing together because Alison was white, and I was Black. After school that day, I went home to ask my mother the meaning of the word the child had shouted at me. My mother shared the definition that was in the dictionary at the time, and she said I was not, in fact, what the dictionary said. I wasn't a nigger. She went on to talk about history and shared that, at certain points in history, it was commonplace for white-bodied individuals to call Black people niggers. I remember feeling relieved once my mom said I wasn't what that boy called me. In so many ways, all that mattered to me was what my mother thought of me. Her love and care were much more powerful than that boy's words.

I have thought back to that incident several times throughout my life. I have processed different layers of what I experienced, and what I am left with are questions: What made that child call me that name? How did he know the word? Who taught him the word and to use it in the way he did? Why did he say it to me that way and on that specific day? We had already been in school together for two months. What did I represent to him? Why was my very being bothering him so much so that he needed to call me a nigger that day? Why did he hate me so much? Did he hate me at all?

The fourth klesha is dvesha, aversion or avoidance. Dvesha takes root from avidya and asmita and is in deep relationship with raga. Whereas raga is an attachment to pleasure, dvesha is an attachment to that which we believe we do not like. This dislike can easily turn into hate, and in this chapter we will begin to investigate how. Not only is dvesha about the feeling of hatred or having an aversion to certain objects, experiences, or people, but it is also accompanied by the desire to eliminate the object of our aversion or hatred. Similar to raga and how we can become one with our desires and develop an attachment to pleasure, we can also become one with our attachment to hate.

As the Yoga Sutras describe, our minds are affected by mental impressions that shape our perception. Lived experiences, messages, and our cultural conditioning shape these impressions. These mental impressions might be positive—for example, my memory of Cheez-Its and my mother and the joy this memory brings me. It also makes me want to re-create the experience because it felt like such a fun and nurturing experience. As shared in chapter 8, I often wish to eat Cheez-Its when I am not even hungry. In this way, my mind experiences some disruption based on the mental impression formed from the experience of watching television and eating a tasty snack with my mom on Friday evening. This disruption occurs because I confuse what I desire and an attachment to that experience and pleasure or good feelings with what I actually need instead of the Cheez-Its, which, often, is to wind down for the evening and go to bed.

Mental impressions can be negative and create an aversion to someone, something, or an object. For example, I am allergic to watermelon and do not eat it. When I was a child, I ate it, and my grandfather would tell me not to eat the seeds because a watermelon would grow inside me. I would laugh because it seemed impossible to have a seed grow into a watermelon inside me. When I turned twenty, I developed an allergy to it. If I see a watermelon in the store, at a summer barbeque, or on a menu in a restaurant, I have a sensory reaction to it. At times, I start to feel nauseated, but most of the time, I just notice feeling an aversion to watermelon, so much so that it momentarily disrupts my nervous system and mind. Cheez-Its and watermelon are small examples of how our mental impressions are formed and how simple things influence our minds so much so that we develop an attachment to our desire for or aversion to them. Clearly these examples are tame in comparison to someone unconsciously or consciously expressing hate through words like "nigger" on a playground.

When sensory impressions enter the mind, what is called *ahamkara*, defined as our ego or the identity maker, labels or colors the impressions as something we like or dislike. Sensory impressions and ahamkara function to label mental impressions and shape our identity and sense of self. Ahamkara can create a sense of false identity where one confuses what they label as liking or disliking with the whole of who they are. This pattern of confusion can lead one to assume that anything labeled with dvesha, or as aversive, is related to oneself. Ahamkara also labels things as "me" or "mine," meaning we begin to believe our sensory impressions are who we are. Dvesha can also lead us to such an immense aversion to something or someone that we might want to own or dominate it or them; we might also develop such an intense level of aversion to or hate for someone or something that we want to annihilate it.

When I encounter something like watermelon, which I have an aversion to, and for good reason because it makes me sick, part of my sensory response is to want to get rid of the watermelon. I am actually just fine with people eating it around me, but I'm hypersensitive to the fact that it might touch my food and, in response, I could become sick. Every time I see watermelon in the grocery store, I remember I cannot eat it. It's not that I want to get rid of all of the watermelons in the world. I don't let watermelon disturb my state of peace that much. But if I developed an unhealthy or debilitating attachment to my aversion to it, I can imagine seeking to avoid it at all costs out of this extreme fear.

I don't know if the little boy on the playground was conscious of what he was saying, but he knew to say it to me and not the white-bodied children on the playground. I don't know if he understood that he was likely mimicking oppressive behavior by shouting something to me he had probably heard from other students, family, or the media. I do know he was angry, and he didn't want to share space with me or for me to be on the playground. I do know he wasn't happy that Alison didn't co-sign on to his hate and, instead, told him to stop calling me names. The boy had experienced something, maybe many things, that shaped his mind and formed sensory impressions that led him to develop an aversion to me, a Black person, enough for him to spit on me and to call me a "nigger." I won't say he wanted to get rid of me, but he didn't like me and didn't want me to be in the same vicinity as him.

In our lives, we can begin to notice and witness ahamkara. We can notice our response to various people, places, objects, and experiences, and we can notice whether or not things are labeled as enjoyable, unenjoyable, or neutral. We can also notice the intensity of our response to various experiences. We can notice when we label things as good or bad and right or wrong. We can notice if things are beautiful or what we would label as ugly. All of this information is stored in the mindfield, waiting for another experience to reinforce the labeling that has already occurred. Reinforcement of something that is enjoyable can form an attachment, raga. Reinforcement of something that was labeled as unpleasant can form an attachment, dvesha.

The boy who called me a name while I was on the playground saw me as different and labeled me as something bad, wrong, and certainly not someone who was worthy of being on the playground with my friend. The intensity of the mental impression and labeling about Black people being bad, wrong, or unworthy was intense enough for him to stop playing with his friends, use energy to walk over to where I was with Alison, spit, and say something harmful and hurtful to me. The mental impression was so intense and deep that this boy was distressed and disturbed enough to want to disrupt my peace. "*Dvesha* captures and occupies our consciousness so powerfully that we cannot pull the mind away."[11]

Most of us have been mentally conditioned to hold on to negative experiences and thoughts versus positive ones. Here, I will offer a public speaking experience to illustrate how conditioning can contribute to us holding on to negative experiences. Public speaking is part of my work in the world. When I first started to speak publicly and facilitate, I was nervous. My voice would shake, and sometimes I didn't feel equipped to speak. I remember one time I went completely blank while giving a speech during an event for Sexual Assault Awareness Month. At the time, I was working at a rape crisis center. I am a survivor of sexual violence, and being asked to speak during the event felt like an honor. I thought I was prepared to speak, but something about the setting and the stimuli in the space threw me off a bit. I had heard several stories of survivorship from primary and secondary survivors. Then it was my turn to offer words to the group that would support them in feeling grounded and fully integrated as they left the event. I barely remember what I shared during my speech, but I do remember not feeling good about it.

The next day, a co-worker who had been at the event asked me how I felt about my speech. I told her I thought I did a terrible job. In response, she asked me what I thought went well. I could think of one thing that went well, but my mind was preoccupied with the twenty-five things I thought didn't. This is how the mind works. Though the mind does hold on to pleasant experiences as a way of avoiding unpleasant ones, we are more likely to remember negative thoughts and experiences than positive ones. "Yet under the influence of a mysterious force, we appear to treasure unpleasant memories even more than we treasure pleasant ones, although we may not realize it. This mysterious force is dvesha."[12] I didn't stop giving talks or speeches, but as I reflect back on this time when I felt as if I didn't do well giving a speech, I still feel some shame. What is so funny about this example is that, a few years after I gave the speech at the event for the rape crisis center, that same organization asked me to come back and give another speech. I agreed, and it went swimmingly.

Pain as a Resting Ground

Affliction that has pain as its resting ground is aversion.
—YOGA SUTRAS 2.8, TRANSLATED BY PANDIT RAJMANI TIGUNAIT,
THE PRACTICE OF THE YOGA SUTRA: SADHANA PADA

This yoga sutra pinpoints that pain is the resting ground for aversion. Something that feels striking to me about this particular sutra, dvesha, and the story about the child calling me a derogatory name on the playground is that pain is the outcome of oppression as well as the root of oppression. Forming an aversion to something or someone comes from a place of suffering due to how we have been conditioned by dominant culture, our own experiences of trauma and oppression, and the belief that we are separate from one another. We will look into this in much more detail in chapter 11.

After avidya takes root, and we forget that we are *purusha*, pure consciousness, we begin to interact with things that make mental impressions, and ahamkara labels our experiences. This labeling shapes our perception of self and others and our relationship to others. We form an identity based on these mental impressions and become overly attached to various parts of identity and ego, and we form pleasant and unpleasant associations with various people, places, objects, events, and experiences. These kleshas are the breeding ground for the final klesha —abhinivesha, defined as a fear of letting go—which we will explore later in *Illuminating Our True Nature.*

The connection I will make now is that, because of raga, we are drawn to things that we perceive to be pleasurable. We want to recreate these things and are afraid of losing them once we experience them. For example, I have been in romantic relationships that have felt absolutely intoxicating. This intoxication led me to want more of whatever I was experiencing in these relationships, be that fun, deep conversations, or mind-blowing sex. I wanted more of whatever these relationships made me feel, and this also led me to fear losing them. So much so that I would cling to them even when they weren't good for me. As we have explored, dvesha is an aversion to something. Dvesha can lead to a fear of encountering that which one does not want or that which one might label as unpleasant. Once this encounter occurs and one experiences something they perceive as unpleasant, they are afraid of the experience, and the unpleasant feeling is permanent. As discussed in chapter 9, everything we experience is temporary, but fear coupled with an attachment to pleasure or aversion leads to abhinivesha, a resistance to letting go or death.

When the boy called me a name on the playground, it was because he encountered something he perceived as unpleasant. In some way, my being Black was challenging his sense of self. Not only did he see himself as separate from me, he also saw himself as better than me. At its core, dvesha can make us feel such acute aversion that we make an enemy out of whatever we are trying to avoid or dislike. Chapter 11 offers a deeper understanding of dvesha on a collective scale and how it intersects with forces such as dominance, superiority, and oppression. The boy who called me a "nigger" was a microcosm of the macro experience we are all having on the planet at this time.

We live in a world and through a time when hate and separation are prominent. In my experience, the path of yoga brings us back into union with ourselves and one another. The path of yoga is a powerful antidote to dvesha and all of the kleshas. The practice of yoga assists us in noticing our response to various stimuli. Yoga can support us in noticing when we respond from a place of liking or disliking someone or something and understanding when our likes, dislikes, and labels develop into attachments. Yoga also holds the key to us disrupting our attachments that lead to our suffering, through the process of teaching us who we and everyone truly are—pure consciousness. The practice of yoga always calls us into connection versus separation and hate. In subsequent chapters, we will continue to delve into how to engage the practice of yoga to respond to dvesha and the samskaras and obstacles in the way of our liberation.

REFLECTION QUESTIONS

Please reflect on the following reflection questions to develop a clearer understanding of how dvesha is showing up in your life. In the next chapter, I will ask you to reflect on how it is showing up in the collective.

- ▶ Where do you notice dvesha, aversion or avoidance, showing up in your life?

- ▶ What do you believe the relationship is between avidya and dvesha?

- ▶ Where, for you, has dvesha directly emerged from a place of believing you are separate from someone or something else?

- ▶ What is the personal cost to you when you develop an aversion to or avoid someone or something?

- ▶ How can the path of yoga support you in working to notice dvesha and to mitigate the suffering you experience because of it?

11

Made Manifest from Hate

If we fail to address the world's collective trauma with clarity and compassion, we imperil the survival of our children and our children's children—and countless other species.

—THOMAS HÜBL, *HEALING COLLECTIVE TRAUMA: A PROCESS FOR INTEGRATING OUR INTERGENERATIONAL AND CULTURAL WOUNDS*

IN THE PREVIOUS chapter, I shared a story of hate and racism directed toward me. It was just one of many experiences of racism I have endured in my life thus far. It was an incident representative of a more significant divide across lines of race. It was an incident representative of the divide we experience based not just on race but also on other identities we embody, such as gender identity and expression, body size, class, citizenship status, education level, and more. The story shared in chapter 10 directly connects to the concept of social location explored in chapter 5 and the hierarchy of bodies developed by people more proximal to power to maintain their access to social and institutional power. This hierarchy of bodies situates some people in closer proximity to power and some further away. This is intentional, and the pattern and practice of assigning power to a small group of people who are setting cultural norms, as well as defining what and who is normal, is embedded in almost every, if not every, institution and system. This chapter looks at how dvesha is expressed on a collective scale and will connect the experience I shared in chapter 10 with an experience across lines of race and difference that affect many people. This chapter explores the belief that we are separate and the consequences of this belief when coupled with a breeding ground for aversion and hate.

It was mid-May 2022. I was just a few weeks into a three-month sabbatical. I had decided to take some intentional time away from the hustle of life to try to settle into myself. Even as I was settling into stillness and taking a break from Zoom meetings and many of my work projects, I continued to be fully aware the world was still in motion. As I was slowing down, I understood I might become more attuned to the clamorous state of the world. In my consciousness, I had the memory and experience of what had happened just two years prior when many of us were in a state of forced solitude due to the COVID-19 pandemic. The murder of George Floyd against the backdrop of masks, a disorganized response to the pandemic, conversations about who was an essential worker and who was not, bodies being stored in ice-cold trucks in hospital parking lots, and the experience of moving through a level of uncertainty that so many of us had never before faced stirred something in us. In the eeriest of ways, COVID-19 made the world feel quiet to me, and the murder of George Floyd and the global response to it made the world erupt in righteous raucousness.

As I entered my sabbatical, my body, heart, mind, and spirit knew what it was like to navigate an unsettled world while in search of a state of peace. Then, on the evening of May 19, 2022, I heard the news of the shooting in Buffalo, New York. The shooting took place in a Tops grocery store. The grocery store's customer base was predominantly elderly Black people. The shooter was a nineteen-year-old white-bodied man who openly admitted the crime was racially motivated. He planned the attack with the intention of killing as many African Americans as possible. According to his social media account and a document he wrote in preparation for the attack, his precise goals for the attack were "To kill as many African Americans as possible, avoid dying, and spread ideals."[13] The ideals he was referencing are those held by a white supremacist culture that supports the idea that white is superior to Black and all People of Color, People of the Global Majority, and Bodies of Culture.

Upon hearing the news, my heart sank as I tried to make sense of something that seemed senseless. Despite my heartbreak, I continued to move through the evening and prepare for the next day. The next morning, I taught a yoga and meditation practice and wore my Black Lives Matter T-shirt. During the class, I acknowledged the shooting, and the participants in the class and I uplifted prayers for the families, co-workers, and loved ones of the people who were killed in the attack. After class, I realized I needed to head out to the grocery store to grab a few things for a gathering I was hosting at my house a bit later in the day. I went into my bedroom, and as I was heading over to my dresser to grab my keys, I glanced in the mirror. I saw myself and my Black Lives Matter T-shirt, and I almost had a panic attack. I thought, "I cannot go to the grocery store with this shirt on." Then I thought, "I cannot go to the grocery store at all." I sat on my bed and sobbed for a little while, then changed my shirt, grabbed my keys, and went to the grocery store. I cannot say what made me bypass my desire to stay at home and not go out at all. But my response of moving with fear to do the things I need to do, like go to the grocery store, while trying to respond to and manage my racial trauma felt quick and automatic. The truth is, I have had to face many fears that emerge from being Black in America, so I've learned to cope and keep it moving.

While in the store, I had a response that felt familiar to me, a response that has often emerged during similar times of racial unrest. I felt like my Black skin was very evident to everyone I passed by in the store. I wanted to hide. I wanted to scream at everyone who seemed to be moving through the store, unphased by what had happened just a day prior in a grocery store in Buffalo, New York. I wanted to ask shoppers if they were thinking about what happened. I wanted to ask store employees if they were thinking about what happened. I wanted to know if anyone else felt unsafe doing something as mundane as going to the grocery store. Instead of inquiring with fellow shoppers and store employees, and instead of screaming or hiding, I kept quiet and tried to get out of the store as quickly as possible. I imagined what my experience would have been like had I been wearing my Black Lives Matter T-shirt, and I felt enraged that I had known to take it off before heading to the store. But I have lived long enough to know when and when not to stoke the raging fire white supremacy started long ago.

Later that day, I spoke to my mom on the phone. I told her the story of the T-shirt and the grocery store. She said, "You were right to take off that T-shirt." I felt a bit irritated by this, but I understood what she was saying was that I didn't need to bring more attention to myself than my Black skin already did. During the course of our conversation, my mother also shared that she didn't feel like this world was a place for old people. As an eighty-year-old herself, I am sure she was relating to the people who were elders in Buffalo who went to the grocery store never to return home to their families. It is routine for her to share with me how much worse the world has gotten. I don't know if things have gotten worse over time, but I do know things are very polarized and challenging at this time. The political landscape in the United States is rife with corruption, division, and a lack of collaboration across party lines. We have a prevalence of laws that limit the choices people can make about their bodies, and particularly choices for people who are less proximal to power. Anti-trans bills are being introduced at a rapid pace. Climate change is making natural disasters such as tsunamis, hurricanes, and tornadoes stronger and more frequent as well as causing more extreme high temperatures during spring and summer and more extreme cold temperatures in the winter across the globe. This is not natural at all. People do not have what they need to survive, much less thrive. The world feels intense.

The Micro and Macro

The shooting in Buffalo is just one out of many travesties motivated by hate and dominance we are responding to. In the wake of the shooting, I found myself sitting with some of the same questions that always emerge when hearing news of senseless acts of violence motivated by fear, hate, and power. Similar questions to the ones that came when my classmate called me a "nigger" on the playground—questions rooted in wanting to understand how we came to be so violent toward one another; questions rooted in wanting to understand why we are inhumane to one another and to other beings. What has caused us to be so averse to one another? How do we know how to hate one another? How do we learn to hate and oppress one another and the planet? In what ways are we incentivized to uphold systems of oppression and the hierarchy of bodies that exist? What makes one turn their hate into action? How and why do hate and abuses of power manifest themselves? Will we continue to harm one another? What will bring us back to each other? When will we realize that systems of superiority harm us all? What will make us disrupt and interrupt systems of superiority and the hierarchy of power and bodies? As I sat with these questions, I was once again reminded of how everything that is individually playing out for us is also playing out for us as a collective.

As previously explained, dvesha is an aversion to something based on our mind's response to a stimulus and the mental impression that is then formed. Our minds, bodies, hearts, and spirits are influenced and shaped by the various forces that condition and socialize us, such as family, environment, institutions, and culture. This conditioning leads us to create mental impressions in response to those who are just like us and those people who might embody identities different from our own. The way many of us are socialized or influenced by culture is to believe some groups are superior to others. This idea is reinforced within institutions and perpetuated through cultural norms. Therefore, we knowingly or unknowingly develop impressions about entire groups of people and create behaviors in response to these impressions. One of these behaviors is to develop an aversion to people who are different from us and who are less proximal to social and institutional power.

Remember that because dvesha is rooted in avidya and the belief that we are separate, and because this can be so powerful within us, we can develop the desire to conquer or dominate that which is different from us because our aversion is so powerful it can control the mind and our behaviors. This causes suffering not only for us but for the collective. Just as the little boy who called me a "nigger" was so bothered by my very being on the playground when he came over to Alison and me to disrupt our playtime, the shooter in the Tops grocery store was so disrupted by the stimulus of Black people existing that he calculated a plan to go to a grocery store where he knew many Black elders shopped in order to kill them. During the incident, he pointed his gun at a white-bodied man, apologized, and didn't shoot the white-bodied man because the shooter's intent was to harm Black people. He carried out his plan by shooting thirteen people: eleven Black people and two white people. Thirteen people were shot and ten of them died.

This is just one example of a hate crime motivated by separation, the belief that one is superior, and the indoctrination into a culture that upholds dominance, superiority, and a hierarchy of bodies. The incident described in chapter 10 about the white-bodied boy calling me a "nigger" on the playground mirrors what has been and is unfolding related to race relations, white supremacy, and difference in our world. The pattern of mass shootings or modern-day lynchings to rid those who are labeled or seen as undesirable isn't new. The pattern of trying to conquer something we dislike isn't new, either. The forces meant to divide us are old and familiar. The mental impressions birthed from our social conditioning that develop into attitudes of intolerance and aversion are deep. The pathways in our minds that suggest we are better than others, that it is okay to dislike or hate someone or something, and that cause us to feel distressed, disturbed, or uncomfortable are extensive.

In addition to oppression that manifests from white supremacy, other examples of systems that create suffering because of dvesha also create conditions that cause humans to believe they are superior to nonhuman species, superior to the planet; heterosexual and cisgender people to believe they are superior to 2SLGBTQIA+ people; citizens to believe they are superior to refugees; abled people to believe they are superior to disabled people; and so on. Any group that is more proximal to social and institutional power is taught to believe they are superior to those who are less proximal to social and institutional power, thus leading to the formation of mental impressions and the development of negative associations about those who are different from us. This can result in mental disturbances that derive from and continue to perpetuate the hierarchy of bodies. I am not suggesting that if you embody one or more than one identity that is more proximal to power you consciously hate those who are less proximal to power. I am suggesting that we are taught to believe those who are less proximal to power are inferior to us, and this forms mental impressions that lead us to act out of this belief in a way that is harmful to those we believe are inferior.

No matter how cleverly we veil it, dvesha destroys our inner peace. It dulls the brilliance of our mind, damages our faculty of discernment, and deranges our senses . . . It shakes our nervous systems, disrupts the functions of our body, and eventually makes us ill—physically, mentally, and spiritually.
—PANDIT RAJMANI TIGUNAIT, *THE PRACTICE OF THE YOGA SUTRA: SADHANA PADA*

There has been a lot of discussion about mental illness in relationship to the white cisgender men who are responsible for many of the mass shootings that occur in the United States. This discussion has been happening alongside a criminalization of Blackness and a lack of mental healthcare for Black and IPOC people who experience racial trauma and live in a white supremacist culture. I don't know if the shooter in Buffalo was mentally ill, but I do know that his mind was disturbed to the point of wanting to annihilate Black people. I know that systems predicated on the belief that we are separate from one another uphold the hierarchy of bodies. I understand these systems practice divide-and-conquer strategies, deeply affect our minds, and shape our behaviors and the actions we take. These systems lead to the formation of mental impressions that then lead us to be so distressed about difference that we consciously or unconsciously oppress one another and, at worst, annihilate those who we perceive to be different from us. Sometimes this oppression is as blatant and grave as the shooting in Buffalo; other times it can seem more subtle through microaggressions. But whether micro or macro, acts of oppression, aggression, and dominance cause us to suffer and move us away from our humanity.

While I do not personally know the young, white-bodied man who murdered those Black elders on May 19, 2022, I do know he was socialized in a culture that in some way made him believe he was better than the people he chose to murder. I understand that the Black elders he shot and the communities they come from have likely been under the siege of white supremacy for centuries. To release ourselves from the hold aversion and hate has over us, we must understand how hate is truly causing us to suffer—hate that is incentivized by systems of dominance, hate that comes from what we have internalized about who we are in the hierarchy of bodies, and hate from which we believe we have something to gain.

Spiritual Bypassing

Conversations about love and hate, particularly in spiritual communities, are prevalent, though they often lack depth or an understanding that simply being more loving or expressing less hate will not transcend the systems of dominance that are embedded in culture and institutions. While the intention of the eight-limbed path is to move us toward collective liberation, we cannot simply meditate oppression away. Yoga asana can most certainly transform us physically and otherwise, but it will not necessarily transform how people show up in their lives and the postures they embody when encountering discomfort or those who are different from them. Yoga asana will not necessarily cause someone to choose to posture in a different way from how they have been conditioned to shrink themselves or take up more space. A practice of *ahimsa*, non-violence, will be actualized only if those more proximal to power account for the violence they have caused and continue to cause to those who are less proximal to power. A practice of *asteya*, non-stealing, will come to fruition only if we understand the capitalist context we live inside and create new economies and ways of being that aren't based on extraction, consumerism, and productivity over people.

"Spiritual bypassing" is a term coined by John Welwood. It is a term that essentially speaks to the way one becomes addicted to spiritual practice and begins to avoid what truly needs to heal within them. Spiritual bypassing can lead to one avoiding what needs to heal to such an extent that they do not address developmental, physical, or emotional needs. When bypassing is happening, often absolute truths, such as "we are one," are used as a way of avoiding relative truths, such as we do not live as one. Spiritual bypassing is dangerous because it offers an escape hatch for those on a spiritual path. They can escape from the reality in which we live, act as if absolute truths are the only truths in existence, and work to transcend the reality of what it means to be in a human body on the planet at this time. While so much of what Book Two of the

Yoga Sutras offers speaks to how to work with the mind and move closer to the truth of who we are (which is something much greater than the confines of our minds and bodies) through practice and sadhana, I do not believe the intention of Book Two was for us to start from a place of transcendence. That section of the Yoga Sutras assumes we are not enlightened; we are not yet in a place of understanding who we truly are. It offers tools for us to get back to the truth while we are in human bodies so we suffer less both now and when the time comes for us to leave our current incarnation.

The shooter in Buffalo was distressed and disturbed. He was suffering and inflicted suffering on others. Even so, I cannot pray his racism away. We cannot pray his racism away. We cannot pray away his sense of internalized superiority. We cannot act as if being more loving will transform someone whose mental impressions so deeply disrupted them that they planned and carried out an attack. As we work to get closer to God or Spirit, our divinity, and our shared humanity, we cannot bypass the truth of what is unfolding in the earthly realm.

For me, this means that my practice must make me more aware of my mental impressions and what or who I label as bad or wrong. I must interrogate myself and ask myself why I label certain experiences or groups as bad or wrong and investigate my aversions. I need to work to understand what allows aversion to take root and grow. I need to recognize how my aversion to someone or something could lead to further violence and separation. The practice of seeing and witnessing myself will begin to help me investigate and interrogate my conditioning, thoughts, and patterns. This practice can move beyond me and into the groups of which I am a part. Yoga practice allows me to begin to see the narratives I have been told about who I am and who others are and to challenge these narratives when they are in direct opposition to collective liberation. This isn't easy work to do. This is why rigor is important as a practitioner of yoga. It is also important to understand this is a journey. Instead of bypassing the relative truth playing out and the truth of who yoga understands us to be, we can commit to a path of study and devotion that will allow us to move into closer alignment with values, principles, and actions that will lead us to samadhi and to collective liberation.

I recognize the content in this chapter and the previous one may have brought up intense emotions for you. They did for me. The content shared in these two chapters wasn't easy to write, and I imagine for you, the reader, it wasn't easy to read and digest. The reality is we are responding to many forms of trauma originating from our mental impressions, disturbances to the mind, overwhelm, and the cultural context. It seems as if we are surrounded by our own and others' attachments to aversion, or that which we do not like, want to encounter, or confront. The opportunity that emerges from looking at how we experience dvesha individually and collectively is that we can begin to dismantle the dysfunction that an attachment to aversion creates. Dvesha exists in almost every facet of life—in our thoughts that can form biases and in our behaviors, what we express through words, and our actions. The next chapter offers more extensive practices to support you in releasing the hold dvesha might have on you and us as a collective at this time.

REFLECTION QUESTIONS

For now, I would invite you to take a few deep breaths. I invite you to breathe and come back to your body and to notice how you feel. Once you have done this, please reflect on the following questions.

▶ Where do you notice dvesha—aversion or avoidance—showing up in our world within systems, through policies and protocols, and in cultural norms?

▶ How do systems coupled with a hierarchy of bodies incentivize us to continue to believe and operate as if we are separate from one another?

▶ What is the cost to the collective when we believe we are separate from one another?

▶ How can the path of yoga support us in working to notice dvesha and to mitigate the experience of collective suffering?

After you have reflected on the questions listed above, I invite you to set an intention for yourself to more consciously notice how dvesha shows up for you and affects your relationship to self and, as explored in this chapter, the collective. You can sit and take a few deep breaths, then set your intention and repeat it to yourself three times. Hold your intention in your awareness and heart as a way of more fully living into your commitment to better understand how dvesha shows up in your life and to work to decrease the suffering it creates for you and others.

12

Inner Peace

Healing is the building block of both individual and collective
spiritual evolution.

—DONNA GODDARD, *CIRCLES OF SEPARATION*

WHEN I REACHED age thirteen and my body began to move
through the physiological and developmental process of
puberty, my hormones began to shift, and my body started to
retain more water. At that point, I was unaware my mother had lymphedema; her symptoms were nascent. I didn't know why my legs felt like
tree trunks once a month and why water was trapped in them. I did not
understand that my lymphatic system wasn't properly working when my
legs felt this way. Because I didn't know what was happening to my body,
I didn't tell anyone. I assumed it was normal bloating and water retention that can occur for people who menstruate.

Throughout the years, the water retention continued. When I was
around age thirty-nine, it became more intense. At this point, I knew
my mother had a terrible case of lymphedema; her feet and legs were
swollen with stagnant water, and her joints were in pain because of rheu-
matoid arthritis, which she inherited from her mother. She saw specialist after specialist who prescribed diuretics and compression stockings
and resisted ordering a pump for her swollen legs. Coupled with lymphedema, I have a condition called interstitial cystitis. The doctors told me

that my legs' swelling wasn't connected to the inflammation of my blad-der. This didn't make sense to me.

A person whose lymphatic system works well experiences interstitial fluid in their tissues that is then picked up by their lymphatic vessels and returned to the blood. When one suffers from lymphedema, the fluid builds up in the tissues and isn't removed at an optimal rate and returned to the blood. It is considered an inflammatory response. When one has interstitial cystitis, their bladder is inflamed. Water accumulates, making it so one feels as if they have a constant urinary tract infection when, in fact, there is no infection at all. Both of these inflammatory responses in my body are difficult to live with, and over time I became curious about whether or not they were genetic. Each time I would ask a doctor about this, they would simply say no. This never felt accurate to me. The inflammation in my body feels old. It didn't begin with me; I do not believe it began with my mother. I believe it began long ago and its origin story is rooted in a system of enslavement and racial trauma, the polyvagal nerve's response to stress, and the connections between this nerve, inflammation, and our nervous systems. The mapping of my own experience of lymphedema has made me consider the connec-tion between autoimmune responses to sustained stress and what stress, oppression, and ancestral trauma do to the body and a person's entire system—the body, mind, spirit, and heart.

Given the energetic imbalance that exists in my body, I have spent time trying traditional Chinese, homeopathic, and holistic remedies to cool my system. While I have times in my life when my body experiences less inflammation, this disruption of flow and my lymph working well is something I imagine I will reckon with for the rest of my life. The aware-ness of this ongoing reckoning and struggle with my lymph, water in my body, and the proper flow of these things has made me contemplate what will bring my body back into balance. Not just my physical body but my energy body. My whole body. This contemplation, coupled with my desire for us to live in a harmonious world, has led me to consider how the collective body can move from a state of rampant inflammation to a state of peace and calm. The inflammation in my body makes me think of the disruption, subsequent suffering, and imbalance dvesha causes. It reminds me of the intensifying inflammation we have been experiencing related to aversion. It reminds me of how aversion becomes embedded into systems, breeds oppression, and creates harmful conditions for those less proximal to power. These patterns are old, systemic, and in our DNA.

Dvesha occurs due to a stimulus related to that which we do not like. If we become preoccupied with or obsessed with what we believe we do not like or are averse to, this causes inflammation, a niggling in the mind that won't let up and can affect the body, spirit, and our emotional state. If this niggling persists, inflammation (mental, physical, or energetic) increases, and an imbalance occurs in our system. This makes it very difficult to find inner peace. Lymphedema feels similar to me. A flare-up can occur because of eating too many inflammatory foods, an increase in stress in my life, changing conditions in my physical and the broader environment, and more. Too much of any of these things causes my system to become out of balance. My body works to bring itself back into a state of homeostasis and peace when it experiences an energetic or physical imbalance. The intention of removing the obstacle of dvesha is to bring us back into a state of homeostasis and peace so that we aren't disturbed, inflamed, or off-balance, and so we aren't creating imbalance and further disturbances in the world.

Years ago, I was introduced to a framework called the "self-system" by my colleague and friend Vivette Jeffries-Logan. Vivette shared the self-system with our collective of dismantling-racism trainers as a tool to explain what happens to one's system as they internalize messages based on their proximity to social and institutional power and social location. If one internalizes a sense of inferiority or superiority based on their embodied identities, this creates an imbalance in the self-system. The self-system shared with me includes four different parts—physical, emotional, mental, and spiritual. As I learned about the self-system, I saw similarities between it and the kosha system in Eastern philosophy, which includes various sheaths or dimensions of the human and spiritual experience. In the system of koshas, we have a physical sheath, *annamaya*, a life-force sheath, *pranamaya*, a mental sheath, *manomaya*, a wisdom sheath, *vijnanamaya*, and a bliss sheath, *anandamaya*.

The self-system framework explains that, when one part of our system is out of balance, the entire system is out of balance. For example, if I am not caring for my physical body and tending to my physical needs such as food, movement, physical expression, and more, this will affect how I feel emotionally, mentally, and spiritually. The kosha system doesn't necessarily suggest that imbalance happens in the same way as the self-system, but it does suggest that the practices contained within the eight-limbed path of yoga—meant to move us beyond the densest part of the body, the physical sheath—can help us connect with deeper parts of our soul. If we are connected to deeper parts of our souls, we are more able to access our Higher Self and attain enlightenment.

Kosha System Example

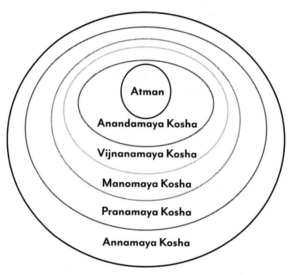

Atman
Anandamaya Kosha
Vijnanamaya Kosha
Manomaya Kosha
Pranamaya Kosha
Annamaya Kosha

The chakra system is another lens through which we can better understand how to move back into balance in response to inflammation or a disturbance. The chakras are energy centers in the body. There are many energy centers, but often only seven are discussed. The chakras represent different parts of our experience, from the root—the base of the spine—to the crown of the head. If there is an imbalance or blockage in one of the chakras, it affects the others. For example, if one has stiffness or pain in their legs or something that disturbs the lower part of their physical body, they may have an imbalance in the root, or *Muladhara* chakra—the energy center associated with earth, grounding, feeling at home, and having one's basic needs met. If someone is experiencing depression or a feeling of disconnection, they may have an imbalance in the third eye, the *Ajna* chakra, or the crown, the *Sahasrara* chakra.

With each one of these lenses and systems, when there is a blockage or disturbance, an imbalance occurs in one's system. When some part of us is off-balance, I believe the other parts of who we are—be that physical or mental, life force or the wisdom body, or the root or heart chakra—are out of balance as well. Moving forward in this chapter, I focus on the self-system as a way for you to better understand how to bring yourself back into balance when you experience a mental impression that colors or imprints someone, an object, or an experience as bad or as something you should develop an aversion to that would cause a disturbance and imbalance in your life.

The Self-System

The four parts of the self-system—the physical, mental, emotional, and spiritual—all correspond to various aspects of our lives. The physical

The Self-System System Example

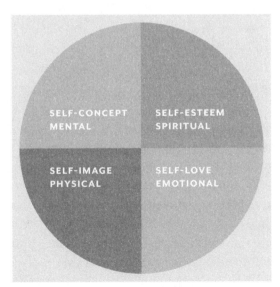

corresponds to the body and our self-image. The mental, the mind and self-concept. The emotional—the various feelings we experience—corresponds with self-love, and the spiritual relates to our self-esteem. Dvesha can affect the physical body and our self-image. If we develop an aversion to someone or something and we develop a belief that we are superior to that which we have an aversion to, we might want to dominate it. This superiority complex may make us develop an inflated sense of self and will most certainly shape our image of who we believe we are and who we are in relationship to other beings.

Emotions that can accompany feeling an aversion for or wanting to avoid someone or something might include dislike, hate, unsettledness, confusion, frustration, distress, and disturbance. These emotions make the mind and body feel distressed until we remove whatever we feel an aversion to or until we successfully situate our lives to avoid whatever has been labeled as negative or bad in our minds. As discussed in the two previous chapters focused on dvesha, the mind is disturbed by a mental impression that codes or colors something as something we should be averse to. If we are not able to work with this mental impression and bring our nervous systems and thought patterns back into a settled state, we might feel so distracted because of dvesha, the aversion, that it takes over our thoughts. Because at its root, all of the kleshas are based in a pattern of forgetting both our interconnectedness and that we all come from the same source—pure consciousness and the Divine. When we are afflicted by dvesha, we may feel disconnected from Source and that which is bigger than us, thus affecting the spiritual part of the self-system. The belief that we are disconnected will cause an imbalance in our system, causing us to replicate a pattern of disconnection. When we are constrained by the belief that we are not spiritual beings, it is much easier to succumb to our suffering and cultivate suffering for others.

The self-system is a tool for us to better understand how dvesha and the other kleshas covered thus far in *Illuminating Our True Nature* are moving us out of balance. The self-system is also a tool to support us in moving back into balance and, ultimately, a place of peace. As you might know from your own experience and wisdom about your self-system, you can likely recognize what happens when your peace is disrupted. Through your engagement with contemplative practices meant to bring you back into peace and equanimity, you have likely experienced moving from a place of distress after a disturbance to your self-system and back into a place of harmony.

Take a moment to reflect on your self-system. Begin by drawing a circle with four quadrants or however many sections you would like to draw to represent the different parts of yourself. After you have a representation of the various parts, layers, sheaths, or energy centers, please reflect on what happens to these different parts of who you are when they are out of balance. What happens to the physical body when you are out of balance? What happens to the mind when you feel off-balance? And so on. Next, reflect on what these parts of yourself feel like when they are in balance. When your spirit is in balance, what does this feel like? Do you feel grounded and more connected to the earth or Source? Do you feel your life force flowing through you freely? When you don't feel as controlled by the ever-changing emotions you experience, what does this feel like? Do you feel more neutral in your response to different events that cause a myriad of emotions to arise?

Now that you've reflected on the self-system more generally, I want you to reflect on it in relation to dvesha. This is a practice you could apply to all the other kleshas as well.

When you consider how dvesha affects your self-system, think of something specific. For example, when I encounter someone who talks too much for my taste, especially when I am in a quiet space, I immediately notice wanting to get away from said person. I have thoughts like, "I wish this person would be more self-aware and notice how much space they are taking up." My body temperature might rise. My thoughts might begin to race, especially if I am unsure of how to get out of the conversation. I might start to feel mad at myself for not being more compassionate, even as I feel highly annoyed by the individual who is talking. When I encounter other scenarios where I feel an aversion to a specific person, group of people, or conditions in my environment, different physical sensations might arise. My thought patterns may be different from yours when you encounter someone whom you perceive is talking too much. We will have divergent experiences in response to dvesha. Take some time to reflect on a specific situation where dvesha has shown up for you and caused suffering for yourself and perhaps others. Reflect on what happened to your self-system in response. Once you have done this, reflect on what practices—such as a deep breath, talking to a friend who can support you in remembering who you are and what you believe, engaging with nature, meditation, mantra, and the like—bring your system back into balance.

A note: The two previous chapters about dvesha explored injustice, oppression, and racial violence. What I am asking you to do now is to take the concept of self-system and reflect on it specifically related to dvesha. I am in no way suggesting that I could've stopped the child who called me a nasty, racist name on the playground with a deep breath, or that a deep breath would have stopped the man who shot and killed people in the Buffalo grocery store. A deep breath would not have stopped either person from acting on their aversion to other Black people or me. I am suggesting that dvesha moves us away from ourselves and causes varying levels of distress, and that it is important for us to recognize what happens to our self-system so we can be more aware of what moves us away from a state of peace and balance. If you feel the desire to use the chakra or kosha system to explore this application of reflection on dvesha and what happens to your self-system, please feel free to do this now or later. This is a practice you can come back to throughout time.

We live in a disruptive world and will encounter suffering in relation to dvesha, be it self-inflicted or because of other people or forces. The practice of yoga is intended to bring us back into a place of harmony in a disharmonious world. It is meant to cool the inflammation in our system. It is meant to support us in creating a peaceful state for ourselves and, ultimately, others.

While my own physical body may live with an imbalance in my lymph system for the rest of my days in this incarnation of myself as I am now, I still strive to feel less inflamed. I strive to imagine and create a world in which my lymph and life force flows freely through me. I strive to imagine and create a world where we can all feel our collective life force flowing freely through us and everything. To me, this would be a beautiful world. A liberated world. A world where we are not bound to our aversions, desires, ego, or the belief that we are separate. A world where we consistently remember what a state of homeostasis feels like. We are not living in this world yet, and we have the practice of yoga to help us come back into a state of harmony and peace. Below, you will find specific practices to support you in removing the obstacle of dvesha and to specifically address how we come back into a state of peace, individually and collectively.

REFLECTION QUESTIONS

How might removing the obstacle of dvesha allow us to heal our collective?

How has your practice of yoga, mindfulness, or any other contemplative practices supported you in coming back into a state of peace after having been out of balance?

Are there examples of when you have been part of or witnessed yoga, mindfulness, or any other contemplative practice supporting the collective or a group in moving back into balance after a disturbance or distressing event?

ASANA

The asana for dvesha is supported bridge pose, *Setu Bandha Sarvangasana*. This posture is a heart opener practiced with the support of props. This allows the heart to open without straining or over-efforting, and this posture can foster an attitude of contentment, *santosha*. This is important as one practices letting go of aversions. Being okay with what is in the present moment while opening the heart and deepening our compassion for ourselves and others is an antidote to dvesha.

Setu Bandha Sarvangasana, Supported Bridge Pose
Variation on Your Back

This posture can be practiced on the floor or in a chair. I will describe how to move into this on a mat on the floor first and then share how to move into it if you are using a chair.

Please have a block, pillow, or set of blankets close by. Begin on your back with your knees bent and placed over your ankles with your feet on the ground, hip distance apart. Place your hands on your belly and take a few deep breaths. You might decide you want to stay here, feeling the support of the earth for several rounds of breath or for the entire time you are in this asana. If you want to add some support under the low back and work to elevate the heart so it is positioned above your head, take a deep breath in and lift your hips.

Place a block on its low, medium, or highest level underneath your low back, or place your pillows or blankets underneath your low back. Take a few deep breaths, and if you need to adjust, please adjust the level of the block or the number of pillows or blankets you might be using for this posture. Allow the low back to rest on the support of your props. Bring your arms down by your sides and gaze at the tip of your nose or beyond, or close your eyes. Stay here for several rounds of breath, noticing how it feels to have your heart supported and, if it is elevated, how it feels to lift your heart higher than your head.

When you are ready to move out of this posture, simply press your feet into the earth, lift your hips, and remove the props so you can place your back on the earth  once again. Take a few deep breaths. Notice how your heart feels and if there is any change in the way you feel physically, emotionally, mentally, and spiritually.

Seated Variation of Supported Bridge Pose

If you would like to move into this posture in a chair, please gather two blocks or supports to place underneath your feet, and a blanket or pillow. The blocks placed underneath your feet can help bring the earth to you and assist you in feeling more supported and grounded. You may not need them, but you can try the posture both ways and see which way feels more accessible.

Sit in your chair, and if you are using the blocks underneath your feet, place them there. Position your knees so they are over your ankles. Now roll up your blanket to make a little pillow for behind your low or middle back. You will place the rolled-up blanket behind your lumbar or thoracic spine (the low or middle back) or somewhere between the low and middle back. In this variation of the posture, your heart will not be elevated in a position that is higher than your head. Once you are settled into your posture, place your hands on your knees, palms face up, or place one or both hands over your heart.

Take a few deep breaths. Notice how this feels in your body, and if you need to make any adjustments with the blocks underneath your feet or the blanket, please adjust them now. Close your eyes or soften your gaze, and take several rounds of breath. Move your shoulders away from your ears. Stay here for as  long as you would like. Once you are ready to move out of the posture, remove the blanket from behind your low or middle back and notice how you feel physically, emotionally, mentally, and spiritually.

MUDRA AND PRANAYAMA PRACTICE

For this practice, you will move through *nadi shodhana pranayama*, alternate nostril breathing. *Nadi* means "channel" or "flow," and *shodhana* means "purification." The mudra and pranayama practices are combined in this chapter. The purpose of this practice is to purify the more subtle channels in the mind and body, or self-system. It can bring balance to your entire system. More specifically, this pranayama practice balances the right and left hemispheres of the brain, balances solar and lunar energy, reduces stress and releases toxins, infuses the body with oxygen, and fosters mental clarity.

Nadi Shodhana Pranayama and Vishnu Mudra

To begin, please decide if you want to practice this in a seated position on the floor or in a chair. Once you have found your posture, take a few deep breaths. Once you feel settled, move into *Vishnu* mudra. This mudra supports one in feeling more balanced and calms the nervous system. Fold the tips of the index and middle

fingers inward until they touch the palm at the base of the right thumb. Your pinky, ring finger, and thumb will be facing up as your

index and middle fingers continue to move inward toward your palm.

Alternatively, you can use your right thumb to close the right nostril and your pinky finger to close the left nostril.

Inhale and use your right thumb to close your right nostril. Exhale gently but fully through the left nostril. Keeping the right nostril closed, inhale through the left nostril and deep into the belly. As you inhale, imagine breath and energy moving up the left side of your body. Pause at the crown of your head.

Now, exhale through the right nostril: Use the ring and pinky fingers of your right hand to gently close your left nostril and simultaneously release your right nostril. Exhale through the right nostril, surrendering the breath down the right side of the body. Pause gently at the bottom of the exhalation.

Inhale through the right nostril: Keeping the left nostril closed, inhale once again through your right nostril, allowing the breath and energy to travel up the right side of your body.

Exhale through your left nostril: Again, use your right thumb to close the right nostril as you release the left nostril. Exhale through your left nostril, moving the breath back down the left side of your body. Pause gently at the bottom of the exhalation.

This completes one round of nadi shodhana. Move through this same pattern for an additional round of nadi shodhana. Then move through several more rounds (5 to 10) of this pranayama practice. When you complete your practice, please exhale through your left nostril and release Vishnu mudra. Relax your hands in your lap or on your knees, and take several deep breaths.

MEDITATION

This meditation is focused on releasing the grip of the things we believe we are averse to while cultivating an attitude of contentment and a compassionate heart.

Releasing the Grip Meditation

Find a comfortable way to be in your body—seated, lying down, or standing.

Once you have found your posture, and if you are seated, place your hands on your knees, the palms facing up or down. If you are standing, you might decide to place your arms by your side.

Close your eyes, or find a soft gaze on the ground in front of you.

Take a few deep breaths to ground and center yourself.

Begin to breathe more deeply, offering a deeper inhale and a longer exhale. Feel the flow of breath as it moves into your body and out of your body.

After several deep breaths, and the next time you inhale, I invite you to bring something that you dislike or believe you have an aversion to—something that is causing you to suffer from dvesha and creating an obstacle in your life, for your self-system, and potentially for others. This could be an object, a person, a scenario, or an experience. On a scale from 1 to 10, 1 being no real aversion and 10 being an intense aversion, I recommend you begin this meditation practice by focusing on something you would classify as a 5 or below. I would refrain from working with systems like capitalism, white supremacy, cisheterosexism, and the like for this meditation because these systems are not rooted in our liberation and will take time to dismantle, more time than this meditation. But, if there is a person or incident connected to these systems representative of how dvesha is showing up in your life, you may choose to work with it during this meditation. If at any point this meditation becomes too intense, please gently move out of it by opening your eyes if they are closed, looking around your space to physically ground, and taking a few deep breaths.

Bring the experience, object, person, or scenario you've chosen to focus on for the meditation into your awareness and notice what happens to your breath. Notice the physical sensations, your spirit, your mind, and any thoughts that might arise. I invite you to notice all you can about it. Take a few deep breaths. Now, in your mind's eye, I want you to imagine turning toward that which you have an aversion to. If it is a person, turn toward them. If it is a sensation you dislike, turn toward it. If it is an experience that left you feeling averse to experiencing that same thing again, turn toward it. Imagine turning toward that which you believe you dislike. You might notice wanting to turn away the moment you turn toward whatever you are working with during this meditation. I invite you to breathe if you notice any resistance to turning toward that which you have an aversion to. Notice everything you can about the person, experience, or focal point for the meditation. Notice the response of what you believe you have an aversion to when you turn toward it. Take a few deep breaths.

Now, I want you to imagine cultivating a different kind of relationship with the object, person, or experience. Perhaps cultivating a relationship that isn't based on aversion or dislike but one that is based on balance, neutrality, equanimity, and compassion. Depending on what you've chosen to focus on for this meditation, this could be a massive spiritual task. This meditation isn't about perfection; instead, it is about cultivating a different relationship with how dvesha shows up in your life so that you feel more liberated and less bound to destroying, avoiding, or annihilating that which you do not like or that which has been labeled or colored as bad or negative based on your conditioning or an experience you have had. Notice yourself, your aversion, and your attempt to have a different relationship with your aversion. If it feels accessible and appropriate, and depending on what you've chosen to focus on, you can reach out a hand in an attempt to connect with the object, person, scenario, or experience.

When you are ready to move out of the meditation, place your hands over your heart and thank your heart for supporting this meditation practice. You may keep your hands on your heart or gently release them as you feel ready. Gently blink open your eyes if they were closed, or lift your gaze. Take a moment to reorient in your space. You might choose to move your body or to ground by scanning your room for comforting objects. You might choose to touch the earth or connect with something in the natural world that you can view outside your window. Come back into the present moment. If you would like to record any observations or insights, please do so now in your journal.

MANTRA

LOKAH SAMASTAH SUKINHO BHAVANTU

Meaning: May all beings everywhere be happy and free.

I have repeated this mantra to myself for at least a decade, maybe longer. I have chanted this mantra because I fervently and wholly believe in our collective freedom and happiness, in our collective safety and wellness. The reason I have chosen to offer this mantra here is that, as you chant this mantra, I invite you to create a world in which this mantra and its meaning come alive in an evident and potent way. This mantra is a full-bodied and spirit-filled prayer for our collective liberation. I invite you to say it at least 10 times, maybe working up to 108 times. Say it with your entire self-system and the whole of who you are. Say it like you believe it is possible and already in motion. *May all beings everywhere be happy and free.* Once you complete your practice with this mantra, record any observations or insights in your journal.

Part Five

Abhinivesha and Letting Go

This section explains the fifth klesha—abhinivesha, or a fear of death or letting go. This section explores how each klesha is interrelated and leads to abhinivesha. It explores norms that lead us to deny the temporary nature of life and the eventual physical death we will all experience, and also provides a larger frame to look at the fear of death related to transition, relationships, the life we thought we would lead, and the like. As I write this section, I am aware that we all have a different understanding of and relationship to death and mortality. The section ends with practices intended to ease our suffering related to death so we can transition with ease and be at peace.

13

Abhinivesha

One of the strange but ever-present states in all beings is the desire to live forever. Even those in the presence of death every day have this illogical desire. This is what inspires the instinct for self-preservation in all of us.
—Sri T. K. V. Desikachar, *Reflections on Yoga Sutras of Patanjali*

THIS CHAPTER INTRODUCES the concept of abhinivesha. The next chapter offers a deeper exploration of why we are afraid of death and what kind of suffering can emerge when we allow this fear to take hold. I have written the chapters in this section through my lens and how I have been shaped by dominant cultural norms, my lived experience, and my spiritual understanding of death and mortality. I have been deeply conditioned by dominant culture and family patterns to shy away from discussing death and mortality. I have been conditioned to act as if death isn't part of life. I have been shaped to process the death of people and not acknowledge the death of anything else. I have been taught that grief related to death is time-limited. I have observed others being unsure of what to say or do when they anticipate the death of someone or when someone shares the news of a recent loss in their lives.

I am aware that people from various other spiritual and faith traditions and backgrounds may have a different experience from what I described above when confronted with death and mortality. Even so, many of us embody patterns that make it difficult for us to let go. Many of us embody patterns based on our shaping that make it difficult to accept death as part of life. Regardless of your faith tradition or spiritual beliefs, it is likely you can point to how a fear of letting go, or a fear of your own death and mortality, has caused suffering for you. It is also likely you can point to patterns emergent in the collective experience we are all having that relate to a fear of death and letting go.

While I understand death is part of life and that, as many people have said before, none of us make it out of here (life) alive, there are times when death happens in a way that doesn't fit the natural order— for example, a child dying before their parents or caregiver; the sudden and unexpected death of someone; deaths from viruses, diseases, cancers, and suicide. The death of our planet due to human behavior and climate change. The death of so many at the hands of systems of oppression. The death of our humanity because of our lack of embodiment. The death of millions due to a virus that was neither predictable nor expected. As you read this chapter and sit with your own relationship to the experience of death, and whatever fear of it may be present for you, please remember there will be times when you as an individual and we as a collective experience the loss of someone or something that doesn't fit the natural order of things as we understand them. It is important to make space for yourself to investigate your relationship with death and mortality while holding space for how you have experienced loss in ways that feel unnatural to you and the universal order of things. I will continue our study of abhinivesha with a story about my birth. It feels fitting to talk about death and a fear of letting go through the lens of birth, because we are constantly in a cycle of birthing and being birthed and of dying and allowing things to die.

While I have not yet fully uncovered a conscious memory of being born into this lifetime, I know being birthed into this incarnation did not come easily. I know this from what has been shared with me by my grandmother, Dorothy, and my mother, Clara. I know this because our cells and tissues remember our birth(s) and death(s). The story I have been told is that I was losing oxygen before I came into this manifestation of myself. The placenta plays a central role in the vital act of breathing. Oxygen is passed through the placenta and umbilical cord. Babies do not take their first real breath until the umbilical cord has been cut. When I was being birthed, and after my mother labored for seventy-two hours to bring me into the world, the doctors discovered I wasn't getting enough oxygen. This means that the conditions in my mother's womb weren't providing me with enough oxygen.

The other pieces of my birth story include the telling of how the placenta emerged before me. After the placenta had been birthed and the doctors determined I was losing oxygen, a decision was made to perform an emergency C-section. This decision was made quickly and without much time for my mother to share her concerns or fears with the doctors or even to process what was happening to her. While she couldn't process the trauma she was trying to survive while birthing me, a baby who couldn't breathe, she also hadn't fully processed the trauma of delivering a stillborn child two years prior to birthing me. The risk of losing me was activating that previous birth trauma, and given that I was signaling it was time to come out of the womb two months earlier than my due date, the stakes were high.

Medically, the placenta emerging before I did suggests that my mother experienced a placental abruption, which is when the placenta detaches from the uterine wall prior to birth. Once this occurs, a baby can suffer severe medical issues, including the loss of oxygen. While I am interested in medical explanations and science, I am also deeply invested in and curious about the great mystery, mythology, shamanic lenses, and stories that have been passed down oracularly from one generation to the next as ways to better understand why certain things occur. I am constantly curious about that which cannot be explained by Western medicine or science and that which can only be explained through a connection to and understanding of Spirit. In many spiritual traditions across the globe, the placenta is revered. In some spiritual practices, how the placenta is handled after it is birthed is a determinant of how a child's life will be. Some spiritual traditions and cultures believe the placenta is connected to the soul.

Many cultures around the world perform special rituals with the placenta. "According to Anne Fadiman, who studied the Hmong tribe in Laos, the word *placenta* is translated there to mean a 'jacket,' which is considered to be the person's first and finest garment. When a Hmong dies, their soul must go back to where the placental 'jacket' is buried and put it on. Only after the soul is properly dressed in the clothing in which it was born can it continue its journey to the 'place beyond the sky' to be reunited with its ancestors."[14] In some cultures, the placenta is believed to be one's guardian angel. "In Bali, the placenta is called 'Ari-Ari' and is considered the physical body of the child's guardian angel, and the angel's spirit stays with the child for life. The placenta is wrapped in cloth and placed within a coconut to be buried."[15] Other cultures believe the placenta is our connection to the earth and ground spirits. "The Igbo tribe of Africa believe that burying the placenta connects the child to the spirits in the ground, and the placenta was given the name 'Our Mother.'"[16]

As I have pieced together a medical and spiritual meaning of why the placenta came out before me during the process of my mother birthing me, I understand that my lifeline to my mother—the person who was responsible for nurturing me while in utero—was prematurely severed when the placenta dislodged from the uterus. I know that it may have been a clearing of sorts for the placenta to emerge before me due to the previous trauma and grief my mother had experienced in birthing a child who never took their first breath. And I know that it was auspicious for my "jacket," guardian angel, and connection to the earth and ground spirits to come out before me.

Shortly after the C-section had been performed, I was pulled out of the womb and brought into this world, then whisked away to a different hospital so my medical needs could be met. The hospital where I was born didn't have a neonatal intensive care unit, so I was taken to the hospital with the most comprehensive care in Richmond, Virginia— what was then known as the Medical College of Virginia (MCV) and is now known as VCU Medical Center. I was at MCV for nine days while my mother lay in Johnston-Willis Hospital trying to recover from a challenging birth and the pain of not physically being near or being given information about me and the status of my health. For her, I imagine it felt as if I were on the other side of the country, thousands of miles away. Often when I recount my birth story, I share that I wouldn't come out of the womb willingly because I was discerning whether I wanted to live this life or not. In part, I believe this was true. I believe my soul, ancestors, and Spirit had some say in whether or not I came into physical form. My choices were to come into this lifetime fully—not knowing the outcome of my life or the journey—or to die, only to be reborn again.

> Even a tiny insect emerging from an egg or pupae struggles to protect its life. No creature needs to be taught about clinging to life and escaping death. This innate tendency to cling to life pervades every living creature.
> —PANDIT RAJMANI TIGUNAIT, *THE PRACTICE OF THE YOGA SUTRAS, SADHANA PADA*

The fifth and final klesha is abhinivesha. *Abhi* means from every direction or point of view, *ni* means complete in every respect, and *vesha* means piercing or penetrating. Abhinivesha is the affliction related to a fear of death that pierces every part of our lives. The reason for this is that the samskaras from previous lifetimes return when we are born or reborn. We are faced with karma created from these samskaras as we live our lives. According to yoga philosophy, the most powerful samskara that returns when we are born or reborn is the memory of dying. I will not presume to know why people die when they do or under what conditions. I am not God and do not have this knowledge. Even so, I do believe a visceral memory of one's own death could make one cling to life.

The Journey to Abhinivesha

> *Fear of death carries its own essence and predominates*
> *[the consciousness of] even the wise.*
> —YOGA SUTRA 2.9, TRANSLATED BY PANDIT RAJMANI TIGUNAIT,
> *THE PRACTICE OF THE YOGA SUTRA, SADHANA PADA*

All of the kleshas explored thus far represent a journey of the human experience rooted in suffering as a result of a fear of letting go and a fear of death. Avidya, ignorance, leads us to believe we are separate entities, disconnected from Source and *purusha*, pure consciousness. As the belief that we are separate takes hold of our experience and understanding of who we are in the world, we begin to cling to the physical and individual experience we have in our human bodies. We forget we are part of a continuum of experience of consciousness throughout all of time and space. We become wedded to staying in our bodies, and our minds are limited due to the belief that we are our individual bodies versus interconnected to all things past, present, and future.

Asmita, our attachment to ego and identities, makes it difficult to let go of one incarnation of who we are now to make way for another. Not only do we become wedded to our bodies, but we also become attached to our ego, the identities we believe represent the whole of who we are, and it becomes challenging for us to see beyond the ego and to live in a way that is in service of the higher consciousness and greater good. Raga, an attachment to pleasure, can breed a fear of letting go because we are afraid the pleasurable things we experience will go away, and we may engage in wanting to recreate pleasurable experiences due to an attachment to pleasure as if pleasure is the only thing that we will or are meant to experience in life. Dvesha, aversion or avoidance, makes us suffer because we become addicted to the aversion toward someone, a group of people, or something. Dvesha intensifies our fear of letting go because of the control our aversion has over us. Our aversions take on lives of their own, so much so that we do not want to die or let go.

The most prevalent form of abhinivesha is fear of our own physical death. Most of us die unwillingly. We do not want to leave our physical bodies. The knowledge that we will leave our physical bodies, coupled with the denial that builds about our eventual deaths, becomes embedded in our cells and tissues, making us cling to life and what we have known. A fear of death and clinging to life are bound together. Many of us are afraid of physical death because, at the time of our deaths, we do not know what will happen, so we cling to life. Even though we are unaware of what will happen when we transition out of our human bodies and this lifetime, on some level—emotional, mental, or psychic—we are aware that, when we transition from the earthly realm and out of our bodies, we will leave everything we have known and lose all we have possessed. We know this because many of us have been faced with loss, be that the physical loss of someone or a transition. We know what it is like for things to die and no longer be available for us to physically touch, feel, see, or be with. Abhinivesha causes us to suffer because we resist the cycle of life. This cycle includes death in one form or another, be that shedding layers, sloughing off identities, alchemy—transforming one substance like wood into ash and ash into a phoenix—allowing things to decay and compost so something new can grow, or an actual physical death of a person, relationship, job, or circumstance.

Abhinivesha relates not only to a fear of physical death but also, more generally, to resistance to letting go of experiences, possessions, memories, identities, egoic tendencies, things that bring us pleasure, and more. It represents the clinging behavior I imagine we all have engaged in at one time or another. At times one may become obsessed with holding on to the life of a relationship, the life of a beloved, or the life of a belief or idea, even if it is causing harm to them. An obsession with holding on instead of letting go creates suffering for us because it skews our perception of reality. We will all die. Everything we have known will die.

Our pervasive struggle with the reality that most of what we know, have, and are experiencing will pass makes it difficult for us to feel free when we are alive because we risk becoming obsessed with maintaining our lives as they are now. We do this so much that we do not truly live our lives nor surrender to the flow of life, which includes death and loss. Our addiction and attachment to how things have been gets in the way of us letting go to make way for something new. Our desire to cling to life as if we are in control of the cycle of life, or of that which will unfold in our lives, causes us to suffer because of the illusion that we have control over what happens and the belief that we can cheat death.

Death and facing death are painful because of losing all we have known, all we believe we are or have been, all we have felt love for, and all we have experienced. Death means facing the unknown darkness of the void. When we are able to learn to let go and allow things to transition and die, we can prepare ourselves to die well. Many different iterations of death will visit us during our lifetimes. We cannot cheat the universal law that change, which includes transition, letting go, and death, is constant, just as birth, life, and rebirth are constant and connected to the limitless flow of our experience as human and spiritual beings.

REFLECTION QUESTIONS

In the next chapter, you will be invited to deepen your understanding of abhinivesha and the cultural norms and messages that make you cling to life, making it more difficult to face death. For now, I invite you to turn toward your breath and to breathe in and out. I invite you to feel the temporary nature of everything as you inhale, pause, and then exhale. The breath is such a teacher about the fleeting nature of most things we will experience on earth. Each breath is connected to all that has been and is now. Each breath is connected to the continual flow of life, and all that will be. Take a few deep breaths, experiencing both the creation of each inhale and the emptying of the breath and the eventual death of each breath cycle at the bottom of your exhale. Breathe here for as long as you would like, staying present to the beauty and fragility of the breath and life. After this practice of conscious breathing feels complete, take some time to respond to the following reflection questions.

▶ How does it feel to know your human body is immortal?

▶ How has abhinivesha shown up in your life related to physical death, transition, and the death of various relationships, jobs, experiences, etc.?

▶ What do you risk when you cling to life or resist letting go?

▶ What practices have supported you in further accepting death as part of life?

14

The Great Paradox

Death is, of course, inevitable, but one of the great paradoxes
of human life is that we usually seem to believe and act as if life
is certain and death is avoidable.
—JUDITH HANSON LASATER, *COMPASSIONATE DYING, YOGA JOURNAL*,
AUGUST 28, 2007

IN NOVEMBER 2022, I had a dream that momentarily disturbed
me. After I had integrated the dream into my experience, I began
to understand it very clearly and how it intersected with the ways in
which we cling to life. I began to consider some of the cultural norms
that have influenced my relationship to death and dying, my mortality,
and my relationship to the finality of my own life, the lives of others, relationships, experiences, and truly, everything I now have and have ever
known. The dream I had was a gift, albeit a jarring one. It assisted me in
better understanding how so many of us are conditioned and socialized
to deny the finality of all that is alive and how this leads us to resist death
as part of life. I want to share this dream with you now.

Dreamscape

We were living on what felt like planet Earth. There were two camps.
One was on the side of "good," and one was on the side of "evil." I was in
charge of the encampment that had an interest in saving ourselves and

the planet, the "good" side in my dream. The other encampment was exploiting resources and people, extracting from the earth, and they lacked a sense of—or rather didn't care about—our shared humanity. I don't know how I came to be in the position of the leader of my camp, but it was clear to me that I was the leader because I was giving directions to folks about various tasks that needed to be completed. I was mapping out a strategy to take over or at least interrupt the other camp.

In my encampment, we had a stone building, some tents in the woods, and tables outside. People were building fires, cooking, gathering weapons (including guns), and trying to gain intelligence from the other side about what they were planning to do. The other camp was located in a school building. This building had two large red doors; the windows were covered so no one could see through them. We would gain glimpses into what was happening inside the school because we had hidden cameras in their building. In some of the footage, I saw something about Facebook, and gathering intelligence and information using Facebook. I saw people crawling around on the floor. I saw people in business suits on their phones and computers sitting at long tables. Some people were interacting, while others were sitting as if they were in the space alone, unaware of what and who was around them. I saw weapons.

At one point, in my encampment, I saw two white-bodied, masculine-appearing people sitting at a red table outside and behind our stone building. They were technologically savvy, and I asked them to look into what was going on inside the other camp. For a moment, I looked away from them to see what was going on somewhere in front of our building, and when I turned back, they were gone. They were there one moment and then gone, vanishing like they had been snatched up by the other encampment. Then, I instructed two other white-bodied, masculine-appearing folks to get their guns and go to the other camp. I instructed them to go inside through the red doors. They got very big guns resembling AK-47s, opened the red doors, and never came back out again. What did come out of the red doors shortly after those two men went into the building were emptied weapons. The chambers of their guns had been emptied.

This is the moment in the dream when I felt myself needing to pivot in strategy and intention. The stakes felt high, and I felt as if we were in great danger. I had to make a move. I grabbed my gray backpack and started walking toward the parking lot. I am not sure where I was going or what my intention was. After a minute or so, I could feel someone walking behind me. I would speed up, and then they would speed up. I had a feeling in my gut that they were going to snatch me as well. I closed my eyes and screamed. The next thing I remember is being in the red school building in a lab. The lab was dimly lit.

I was standing in one part of the lab watching someone who was supposed to be me being suspended in the air. Not too high, but my feet were off the ground. As I witnessed myself, I could tell the people in the lab were doing tests on me. They were experimenting on me. They were doing tests with intense heat to see how much heat I could endure. As I watched myself, I contemplated why they would be doing such an experiment on me. After a few minutes of watching them test my endurance, I asked them what they were doing. Two people in white coats revealed a jar with a serpent in it. The serpent looked like a cobra; it had frog-pond green eyes. They told me they are using DNA to prolong life. They said, "This snake is 906 years old."

I was confused about why any serpent would or should live for that long and about why they were prolonging life. Something felt very ominous and strange about this scenario. Astonished by what they were doing, I said, "Everything is supposed to die. What you are doing is unnatural. Things aren't meant to live forever." They didn't seem to care about my observation of what I perceived as unnatural behavior. They didn't seem to understand what I knew—everything is in an infinite alchemical process of being manifested, birthed, living, dying, and in some spiritual traditions, being reborn. They continued their tests, and when I realized they were planning to continue to test my endurance using different elements including fire, I said, "You can do whatever you want to me, but I will not surrender." I was not going to surrender to the belief that prolonging life was aligned with the universal order of things as I understood them.

My conviction about my belief that we are, in fact, engaged in an infinite alchemical cycle of manifestation, birth, life, death, and rebirth is a testament to my desire to flow with, and my belief in, the natural cycle of things. After stating that I wouldn't surrender several times, I awoke from my dream. When I awoke, I observed my sheets all over the bed as if I had tussled with someone during the night. My sheets were also covered in sweat. I felt unrested. I felt unsettled.

Sleep deprived and a bit distressed from my dream, I rose out of bed and got ready to teach the second day of a Finding Refuge retreat focused on grieving, ritual, and ceremony. During the retreat, people bore witness to their own and others' grief. Retreat participants grieved the loss of people, furry companions, transitions, relationships, health, and more. They acknowledged the infinite cycle of life and death and tended their hearts in community with one another. The morning after my dream, as I was teaching the retreat, I asked participants to get into small groups to share in response to a journal prompt. As they were in small groups, I sat and tried to summon energy while simultaneously continuing to feel haunted by my dream. As I sat, I thought about abhinivesha. I considered how a fear of death, one's own or someone else's, can lead to taking measures to prolong the life of someone or something. I reflected on how an obsession with a fear of death shifts one's mind, thought patterns, and behaviors and how this can lead to a shift in one's own perception of their self and relationship to mortality. This shift in perception can also lead to a shift in how one perceives the outer world.

The truth is, we receive cues about death from the broader culture all the time. Of course, this is largely dependent on where you grew up and norms about death and dying associated with your culture. I grew up in the United States, and while I have studied and infused Eastern traditions and practices into my own life—related to death and many other life experiences—still, I have been largely influenced by Western American culture. This culture has taught me to plan for life as if death isn't part of it. I have been taught to get life insurance, which is a privilege to be able to have and a good thing to have for those I will leave behind so they can feel less burdened with finances after my passing, but I have not been taught to talk to my beloveds about my wishes or desires upon my passing. Culture has taught me not to talk about death but instead to avoid this topic of conversation. It has taught me not to acknowledge death, be that of my goldfish who died when I was five or my grandparent who died when I was ten. An internalized fear of death is present in how we talk or don't talk about death.

If we can, some of us prepare for death, sharing details of how we want our bodies prepared for burial or cremation, how our finances and assets should be handled, and what we desire to happen to memorialize us through a service or ceremony. More often, what I have witnessed is a desire to avoid a conversation about our physical death at all costs, as if we can bypass death. I have been taught to cry at the funeral but to stay strong for my family and those left behind after someone passes. Western culture teaches us not to grieve death but instead to get over death. We are taught to whisper the names of terminal illnesses or the people who have been diagnosed with them instead of affirming illness and sickness as part of what we experience as humans. Western culture teaches us that life is in our control and that to acknowledge our mortality would be an acknowledgment of how much we aren't in control. And we must stay in control.

Cultural norms around defying mortality are embedded in institutions. Healthcare professionals have both been taught to prolong life even when they understand that isn't in the best interest of the patient. Hospice is something one might have to request if they are not lucky enough to be referred to a hospital social worker or healthcare professional who is comfortable talking about hospice and the loving act of making someone comfortable as they face death. Norms around beauty and youth housed within industries, such as the wellness industry, entice us with tonics, tinctures, herbs, and the like in an effort to keep us young and healthy versus facing our own aging process and grappling with our guaranteed and eventual mortality. Political responses to things such as global pandemics highlight the reality that some of us have been conditioned to believe we are invincible, that we will not die, and that we can overcome anything that might come our way, as if our physical strength and ability can outsmart death. We cannot outsmart something like death, and when we believe we can and hold on to life as if it is rigid instead of dynamic and ever-changing, it is difficult to live a liberated life.

Abhinivesha blocks our pathway to liberation because when we are so mired in ego that we cling to life; we suffer because we believe we can conquer death. This makes dying or allowing things to die much more difficult. In my experience, it is not always easy to rise above ego and be with the realization that I cannot conquer death, but when I have faced death or the need to let go and been able to hold faith in something bigger than myself, surrender, and trust Spirit, there has been some relief and more acceptance of whatever is dying in my life at the time. This is why the path of yoga is essential.

The path of yoga teaches us to deal with the pain we might encounter as we face the void. The path of yoga is meant to support us in living a more liberated life and to release this physical world and our bodies when it is time for us to leave them. The practice of yoga prepares us to face life and death, to die well, and to be in the infinite flow that all life presents. It teaches us that the soul is everlasting. We are bigger than our fear of death and the eventual death(s) we will experience. When we forget the magnitude of our souls and their everlasting nature, we limit ourselves. When we remember our divine nature, which cannot be fully contained in or expressed through a physical body, we expand. Our spirits expand. One goal of the practice of yoga is to rid ourselves of our affliction of a fear of death and to release all that might block our ability to fully surrender, to let go so we can feel and be freer in our lives on earth.

The knowledge and expression of death as part of life during the dream I had doesn't mean I am enlightened or that I do not struggle with holding on to things, resist letting go, or fear my own death or the death of things in my life. I understand that I, like everyone else, will transition out of my body and into some other form. I don't presume it will be painless, although the human part of me hopes that it is. The spiritual part of me knows that traversing the darkness of the void and the unknown is not usually painless, but the practice of yoga has equipped me to face and respond to pain. The path of yoga presents a map full of practices that give me the opportunity to practice feeling liberated now, so I can feel truly liberated when I leave my body. The path of yoga teaches that, once I do leave my body, and if I have learned all I need to know and resolved karma, which is highly unlikely, I will be self-actualized and absorbed into the cosmic and greater consciousness. If I have not learned all there is to know or resolved my karma, then I will return and be reborn, given another opportunity or many, to work through the samskaras that cause suffering.

> When life comes to an end, death comes to life. In the realm of death we are enveloped by fear. Birth gives us the opportunity to free ourselves from this numbing affliction.
> —PANDIT RAJMANI TIGUNAIT, *THE PRACTICE OF THE YOGA SUTRA, SADHANA PADA*

There is a similarity between the darkness we face in the void of our passing and that which we face when we are about to be made manifest and in the birth canal. It is the space between the inhale and exhale, the space of potential and the divine spark that helps us traverse in our passing or birth. It is the space where we are reminded of the continual flow of creation and life. Your real-life experiences of death and birth, as well as your association or relationship to the cycle of birth and death, may make it difficult to wrap your head, heart, and spirit around the concepts presented in this chapter. To be in the flow of it all can feel difficult, and in so many ways, this is why abhinivesha is the fifth and final klesha and the most difficult obstacle to work with and try to break through. As we work with this klesha, we are being asked to be in our human form and the earthly realm while embracing that we will not be here in this form and realm forever. This is a painful truth and realization. What I will offer is that the path and practice of yoga can help us be more fully with this truth and realization. The next chapter will offer practices intended to support us in working to decrease abhinivesha.

REFLECTION QUESTIONS

For now, return to your breath and take some time to reflect on the following questions in preparation for the practices in chapter 15.

▶ What messages did you receive about death and dying from your family?

▶ What messages have you received from the broader culture, be that institutions, religion, philosophy, and cultural norms and messages about death and dying?

▶ Have you experienced or been exposed to people or groups of people who willingly acknowledge mortality and death as part of life? If so, what was your experience like with these people or groups of people?

▶ What parallels do you draw between the darkness of the void and the womb of creation?

▶ How has your spiritual practice prepared you to let go and, when it is time, to die?

▶ How does it feel to contemplate these questions?

15

Melt into the Sun

For what is it to die but to stand naked in the wind
and to melt into the sun? . . .
And when the earth shall claim your limbs, then shall
you truly dance.
—KAHLIL GIBRAN, *THE PROPHET*

WE ARE HERE NOW. We have arrived at the final chapter of *Illuminating Our True Nature* and the final set of practices whose intent is to allow you to fully let go into the great beyond, the space of release and letting go. The space of not knowing or needing to know. For this chapter, I will return to a lesson I offered in chapter 6, "From I to We." The theme offered in chapter 6 was focused on the honeybees, and while I didn't anticipate writing yet another chapter about them, they offered a lesson to me about abhinivesha and the cycle of life too poignant not to share. This feels timely for many reasons, one of which is that when we transition, we journey from this realm to another with the hope of being absorbed into all things and returned to our natural state of pure consciousness. We become one with all things in what is likely the most profound journey one can experience—a journey from a place of suffering due to believing we are separate to a deep abiding space of knowing we are part of everyone and everything. A deep abiding space of love.

On the eve of the winter solstice of 2022, I had a dream about my two remaining hives, which I had named Tenacious Bee and Sting. In the dream, they were on their stands in my backyard. I had straps for each hive to strap their hive boxes together and to seal their hive from winter weather. I turned away from them for a moment, and when I turned back around, they were gone. I went searching for them everywhere. I started to ask people if they had seen my beehives, and no one had seen them. They were gone. I was confused about where they could have gone and struck by how fast they had disappeared.

I awoke from my dream, told my partner about it, and went out to the hives to see if I could hear them. I thought I could. We were expecting unseasonably cold weather the weekend after the solstice, and my partner and I prepared the hives by wrapping them in bee cozies to insulate the hive boxes. We weathered the wind that made us chilled to the bone, and we worried about the bees. After the arctic air blew through, I went out to the hives, and once again, I thought I could hear them. I thought I could hear a low hum. A hum that let me know they were in their hive alive, warmed by their collective body heat in the cluster they had formed. After the unseasonably cold winter weather, on a sunny 40-degree day, I fully expected to see Sting, my oldest and biggest hive, flying around. It was routine for them to fly in and out of the hive on cold days, gathering pollen from the camellia bushes, in late December and January. When I didn't see them, I knew something was wrong. I also knew something was wrong because my dream had told me they were going to vanish and were preparing for a journey, strapped in for safekeeping.

On December 30th, my worry and curiosity got the best of me, and I went into both hives and discovered the hives had not been able to survive the extraordinary weather. It was clear they had frozen because in one hive the frames of honey were frozen. In Sting's hive, the frames weren't, but they were rather cold. In Sting's hive, I saw a small cluster of bees that must have hung on until the end, when they were simply too cold to move their bodies and heat their cluster. I was very sad about losing both hives, especially Sting. They have been a hive that has taught me so much. They have been loving to me even when I haven't known what I was doing and haven't tended to them well because of my lack of knowledge. They have been forgiving of my mistakes and have made the most medicinal honey I have ever tasted, year after year. Sting has swarmed around me three times, filling the air with a vibration that moved my spirit to tears because of the magic and wonder of being enlivened by a healthy and vibrant hive. They have been abundant and bountiful in their offerings to me and the greater world. They have been teachers and guides to me.

After I discovered the hives were no longer here in physical form, I cleaned up Tenacious Bee's hive, and Charles harvested the honey, which mead will be made from. Sting's hive was much larger than Tenacious Bee's, and we didn't have time to process all of the frames before we had to head out of town for New Year's. We took the frames of honey from their hive and froze them for future bees that will become part of our bee family in the spring, and we left Sting's hive boxes on their hive stand. When we returned five days later, we noticed something I didn't expect to see. We noticed bees flying around the side of the hive as if they were looking for a way in. I realized that these bees were trying to get in to gather resources for their own hives, so I added an inner cover, which has a hole in it, so the bees could get into the hive and begin to gather nectar, any honey that may have been left in the hive, wax, and propolis. Bees kept coming for days, and days turned into weeks. On a 60-degree day, there were hoards of bees buzzing about the entrance of Sting's hive. When I would put my ear up to the hive, I would hear what sounded like a construction zone, buzzing and drilling. When I stood in front of the hive, I would smell the sweet smell of propolis. When I would touch the entrance of the hive, I would feel the stickiness of the propolis as bees passed in and out of the entrance with sticky propolis on their feet.

It felt strange to mourn Sting while their hive body was still in my yard. It felt as if I was engaging in the death ritual of sitting with and visiting the body. As I would visit, other bees would interact mostly with the hive but sometimes with me, buzzing in my ear or landing on my leg for a spell. This process of facing the transition of a hive and its once vibrant earthly life while also engaging with bees who are still here on earth, and who are gathering resources for their hive from Sting's, was a lesson in both letting go of life and engaging with the living. I was mourning the loss of my beloved hive and feeling my heart fill with awe and wonder at the bees coming to visit what was once Sting's body and what will be another hive's resource.

I was mourning the loss of my beloved hive, and not just the loss of them but about the climate conditions that led to their death, conditions that we have created because we believe we are separate from one another and the planet. Conditions that emerge only from forgetting our true nature and that we are nature. We are every flower, raindrop, honeybee, crow, hummingbird, gust of wind, grain of sand, oak leaf, acorn, blade of grass, berry, river current, butterfly, sunrise, full moon, and star. We are not separate. I was mourning the loss of my beloved hive and also what gets in the way of us realizing this life and all we experience in it is temporary. All we experience in our bodies is temporary; we have to be mindful of how we engage, and we have to commit to decreasing the suffering we and others experience as well as the suffering we cause the earth and all parts of the ecosystem to experience.

Abhinivesha is about removing our fear of death, and in large part, we can do this by remembering the cycle of life. When faced with the stark contrast of life and death in real time, as I was with Sting and the bees who came to sit with me and Sting's former hive, we can let go because we realize our souls are everlasting. We are not our bodies, emotions, egos, or desires. We are the holy hum, the vibration that can be heard from a hive when you are close, or it is close to you. We are the whale song. We are the coyotes singing in celebration of a kill and food for their clan. We are the wolves howling at the moon. We are tree roots communicating with other trees and sending aid when needed to forests near and far. We are fungi and a magical mycelial network. We are sunlight. We are source. We are souls intermingling. We are souls who are everlasting. Sting's soul is now in every particle of air that is flowing through the cosmos at this time. The body where its bees lived is still present in my yard, as the form they are in has transitioned to be omnipresent. This is true for us as well. Letting go isn't just about releasing; it is also about becoming something much more expansive than a body could hold. Letting go is about remembering and returning to. It is about getting free.

As you face your fear of letting go of this life or some part of your life, I remind you that in the process of letting go there is freedom. When we let go, we aren't bound by our bodies or the conditions in place. When we let go, we aren't grasping onto things that do not serve us as individuals or the collective. When we let go, we trust and surrender to Ishvara, God, Spirit, the Divine, or whatever you call that which is bigger than you. We surrender to that which is holy and constant. When we surrender our actions to Ishvara, we devote our lives to that which is bigger than us. We create a world with less clinging and instead more freedom for all.

When we take action from the place of knowing we are everything and everyone while also practicing discernment due to the identities we embody, we can create a world where freedom persists. We can leave our bodies with less fear, knowing that our legacy will live on in soul, spirit, the heavens, and the earthly realm. The reason why I think it is important for us to let go and recognize that this life is temporary is because I believe this will support us in making different choices in our lives.

Karma derives from our afflictions. Karma arises from our unwillingness or our willingness to work through what we are afflicted by. Karma comes with us when we are born and reborn until we work to resolve our afflictions. I don't presume to have a ten-step plan about how we can resolve our afflictions in one or many lifetimes. But I do commit to the path of yoga because it will allow me to learn how afflictions affect me and others, and I engage with the path of yoga to find balance and create balance in the world. I will move on this path of yoga as a devotee and student to learn more about what healing the collective could look like and to heal my own heart so I do not perpetuate samskaras that cause further suffering. I will devote myself to that which is bigger than my human experience. I will pray to my Ishvara and lay my head at their feet again and again. I will ask for guidance, and I will listen to what they share with me.

Below, I offer practices to support you in working with abhinivesha and releasing the grip this klesha may have on you and the role it may play in your life. After the practices, I bring us back to the eight-limbed path and specifically Kriya Yoga as a way of working to remove our afflictions, samskaras, and journey on a path toward samadhi.

REFLECTION QUESTIONS

Reflect on the following questions.

▶ How does the practice of releasing our fear of death and letting go contribute to and create conditions for liberation for us, each other, and the planet?

▶ What have you learned from being faced with the stark contrast of death and life in real time?

▶ How can the eight-limbed path of yoga support you in releasing a fear of death and letting go?

▶ What will you intentionally practice to continue to remember your soul as everlasting?

MUDRA

I begin this set of practices differently than other sections of the book. I begin with the mudra and will end with a mantra. You can choose to move through these in whatever order makes sense for you, but given the flow of practices and particular focus for this section of the book, abhinivesha, I suggest you move through the practices in the outlined order a few times and then adjust or change the order if you would like to do so.

Abhaya Mudra

The mudra for this section is Abhaya mudra. This mudra is considered a gesture of fearlessness. It is a mudra that can support one in dispelling fear and allows one to connect to divine protection. To begin, find a comfortable seat either on the earth or in a chair. Take a few deep breaths and begin to relax into your seat. Place your left hand at your left kneecap with the palm facing upward. Bring your right hand close to your chest with the palm open and facing forward. Your fingers can be upright and your thumb can be tucked in a bit. You can either leave your eyes open or closed as you bring your awareness to your breath. Hold this mudra for at least 5 to 10 minutes. If your arm begins to tire, you can release the mudra and move back into it. When you are ready to release the mudra, gently release and notice how you feel. You can practice holding this mudra, working up to 20 minutes.

ASANA

The asana practice for working to reduce abhinivesha is *savasana.* This is a posture that is often offered at the end of an asana practice as a way of allowing for the integration of the physical practice and also to practice letting go of the mind and body. This posture stimulates the parasympathetic nervous system and calms the sympathetic nervous system, allowing us to come back into a state of homeostasis and balance. This posture is also a simulation of death and what it might be like for us to experience our last breath. This posture isn't practiced to cause anxiety about death and letting go but instead offered as a way of connecting with our aliveness now and the fullness of life with an awareness that life is temporary. Both. And. Life and death. As one teacher taught me once, this is the posture where we go to die and shed that which we no longer need. It is the simulation of death and dying as well as full release of control. It is a posture that supports us in just being, not doing or fixing but just being as we are. Still.

Savasana, Corpse Pose

To prepare for the posture, you might want a blanket, pillow or bolster, eye pillow, and any other props that will allow you to settle into the pose. Savasana is usually practiced on the earth, and you could practice in a chair if that would be more comfortable and accessible for you. If you are going to practice this pose on the earth, roll out your mat or a blanket, and lie on your back. Allow your legs to move to the edges of the mat, and fully relax your legs and feet. Tuck your shoulder blades underneath your back, and allow your arms to move away from your body toward the edges of the mat. If you would like to place a bolster or blanket under your knees or underneath the back of your legs, you can do so. If you would like to cover your body with a blanket, please do so. To withdraw the sense of sight, you might choose to place an eye pillow over your eyes. Stay in this posture for at least 10 minutes if not longer. The mind might tend to wander to other things, especially if you are practicing savasana on its own and not connected to other asanas.

Please feel free to move through the other postures presented in each section of *Illuminating Our True Nature* prior to moving into savasana if this will better support you in settling into rest. When you are ready to move out of this posture, you can gently reawaken your body. Take a deep breath in and out. Gently begin to wiggle your fingers and toes and turn your head from side to side. When you feel ready to take bigger movements in your body, you can bend your knees and place your feet on the floor. Allow your knees to fall to the right side. This will open the left lunar side of your body, which is the side often connected to receptivity, water, and cooling energy, which is what savasana engenders—cooling and calm energy; a state of equilibrium. As you lie on your right side, feel your body here and prepare to rise once again. This part of the practice is often referenced as the fetal position, and when we rise up again, we are reborn. We have experienced what it is like to release the mind and body and are coming back into the body and our lives as we rise back into a seat. Take a moment to sit in meditation. From this point, I invite you to move into the next section, meditation and pranayama.

MEDITATION AND PRANAYAMA

The meditation and pranayama practice are combined in this section. For the meditation, you will sit and breathe mindfully. The practice is to sit with yourself and to be as you are while staying mindful of your breath and present to the moment. For the pranayama practice, you will practice *anapanasati pranayama*, mindful breathing. If you found a comfortable seat after coming out of savasana, please stay in your seat. If you need to adjust to place a blanket or prop underneath your seat or to sit in a chair, please adjust your posture. After you have found a comfortable seat, place your hands on your knees with the palms facing up. Take a few deep breaths and settle into your posture. As you sit, begin to listen to the natural flow of your breath. Begin to feel the rise and fall of your chest. Feel the building of breath in your body as you inhale and the release as you exhale. As you tune in to the breath, notice what else is building in your physical and energetic bodies, and what is building in your spirit. Notice what is being released physically, energetically, and spiritually.

Become a mindful observer of your experience. This mindfulness is what we need to foster if we are to feel less afflicted by our tendencies, samskaras. Mindfulness is what we need to cultivate to feel at peace and practice *santosha*, contentment. Continue to breathe here for at least 10 minutes, mindful of your breath and the moment, meditating and becoming the seer of your own experience. When you feel ready to move out of meditation, take a deep breath in and open your mouth to exhale completely. Gently blink open your eyes and return to your space.

Mantra

TADYATHA OM GATE GATE PARAGATE PARASAMGATE BODHI SVAHA.

Gone, gone, gone beyond, gone beyond the great beyond.

I was introduced to this mantra in a yoga asana class many moons ago. When I heard the teacher chanting TADYATHA OM GATE GATE PARAGATE PARASAMGATE BODHI SVAHA, something about their voice and the words that make up the mantra soothed my spirit. After class, I went home and looked up the mantra and its translation. This mantra is known as the heart-calming mantra. The translation is "Gone, gone, gone beyond, gone beyond the great beyond." This mantra can also be translated to "Gone beyond the great beyond to the other shore, O hail." Or "Gone to the other shore to enlightenment." These translations sunk into me, softening my rough edges. This mantra was like soft water washing over me. I offer it here for you to say, chant, or sing silently to yourself or aloud, alone or in community with others. It is an acknowledgment that we will all travel to the other shore and beyond this earthly realm. It is an acknowledgment we have an opportunity to traverse the waters to travel to the other shore and toward enlightenment and true freedom. To me, this is what my honeybees did. They traveled to the other shore and to a space of pure consciousness, while their spirit is felt here. Always and forever. Now, allow yourself to travel.

Please find a comfortable seat or posture. Place your hands on your knees with the palms face up. Relax your shoulders. Take a few deep breaths and begin to repeat the mantra: TADYATHA OM GATE GATE PARAGATE PARASAMGATE BODHI SVAHA.

The Path Moving Forward

To close this chapter and text, I invite you to come back to how *Illuminating Our True Nature* began. It began by outlining the eight-limbed path of yoga. In Book Two of the Yoga Sutras, Patanjali teaches not only about the kleshas but also what will support us to feel less afflicted and more free. To become the witness and seer of our experience and the experience around us. Patanjali teaches us practices similar to the practices in this book to assist us in feeling less bound to our bodies and, instead, feeling into the expanse of our nature. This is taught through each sutra within the entire Yoga Sutras, while specific practices are offered in Book Two related to the eight-limbed path.

> The practice of the limbs of yoga destroys impurities thereafter, knowledge continues to brighten all the way to *viveka khyati*, the domain of unshakeable discernment.
> —YOGA SUTRA 2.28, TRANSLATED BY PANDIT RAJMANI TIGUNAIT IN *THE PRACTICE OF THE YOGA SUTRA: SADHANA PADA*

As shared in chapter 2, the first klesha is avidya, the belief that we are separate from others. Avidya is the root cause of suffering, and the other kleshas emerge from avidya. When we are no longer afflicted by avidya, our sorrow and suffering will cease to be. As this happens, *viveka khyati* (unshakable discernment) or *prajna* (wisdom) arises. When we connect to prajna, the Yoga Sutras teach us, we can attain freedom from our previous actions and their consequences. Our mind is transformed to a pure state, one that is identical to the purity embodied in Ishvara. This transformation to a pure state with a purified mind is what is called the essence of *mahat tattva*—or the junction of matter, *prakriti*, and spirit, *purusha*. In the Yoga Sutras, the merger of matter and spirit is yoga. Matter and spirit come into union with one another. To be able to merge matter and spirit, we must practice ridding ourselves of our samskaras.

As outlined in chapter 1, Kriya Yoga is *tapas, svadhyaya*, and *Ishvara Pranidhana*. These components of the path of yoga constitute the heart and soul of yoga. When consistently practiced, these components of the path of yoga allow us to serve the purpose of our soul. This is quite different from serving the purpose of our desires, serving from a place of separation, or serving the purpose of our egos, likes, and dislikes. This is about allowing the path of yoga, and our devotion to it and the collective healing of all, to help us reach a collective state of samadhi.

As I close out this chapter, I invite you to return to chapter 1 and the eight-limbed path of yoga outlined in that chapter. I invite you to engage in the path and practice, not as a way to bypass the truth that we suffer and the truth about why we suffer. I invite you to engage the path and practice of yoga to be with the multiple truths we face as we begin to understand why our suffering takes root and contemplate how to get free from our suffering, individually and collectively. I invite you to work toward a place of feeling less afflicted and instead to feel less encumbered and more free, and I invite you to do this in service of the collective good. I also invite you to use Book Two of the Yoga Sutras as a guide to support you in reaching a state of purity, illumination, connection, and enlightenment. It has been my honor to be your guide on this journey through *Illuminating Our True Nature.*

> May you return to this text and the teachings contained in it
>   time and time again.
> May you be safe on your path.
> May you be reverent.
> May you know you are infinitely connected to all that has been,
>   is now, and will be.
> May you find peace.
> May you melt into the sun and, when it is time, dance with Spirit.
> May we all find peace, melt into the sun, and dance with Spirit.
> This is my prayer.
> I will hold it close to my heart as I journey forward on this path
>   of life and yoga.

Notes

1. Diana Raab, "What Is Spiritual Bypassing?" *Psychology Today*, January 23, 2019, https://www.psychologytoday.com/us/blog/the-empowerment-diary/201901/what-is-spiritual-bypassing.
2. Pandit Rajmani Tigunait, "What Are Samskaras and How Do They Affect Us?" accessed August 8, 2023, https://yogainternational.com/article/view/what-are-samskaras-and-how-do-they-affect-us.
3. Meesha Sharma "Practicing the 8 Limbs of Yoga Will Help You Understand Yoga as It Was Meant to Be," *Healthline*, July 7, 2021, https://www.healthline.com/health/fitness/the-8-limbs-of-yoga#history.
4. Padjit Ramani Tigunait, *The Practice of the Yoga Sutra: Sadhana Pada* (Honesdale, PA: Himalayan Institute Press, 2017).
5. Tigunait, *The Practice of the Yoga Sutra*.
6. Tigunait, *The Practice of the Yoga Sutra*.
7. Cynthia Vinney, "Freud: Id, Ego, and Superego Explained," ThoughtCo., February 27, 2019, https://www.thoughtco.com/id-ego-and-superego-4582342.
8. Tigunait, *The Practice of the Yoga Sutra*.
9. Swami Jnaneshvara, "Traditional Yoga and Meditation of the Himalayan Masters," accessed August 28, 2023, https://www.swamij.com/yoga-sutras-10511.htm.
10. Alice Walser, "Fannie Lou Hamer," *New York Times*, April 29, 1973, https://www.nytimes.com/1973/04/29/archives/fannie-lou-hamer-cant-hate-anybody-and-see-gods-face.html.
11. Tigunait, *The Practice of the Yoga Sutra*.
12. Tigunait, *The Practice of the Yoga Sutra*.
13. Mark Morales, Eric Levenson, and Kristina Sgueglia, "Buffalo Grocery Store Mass Shooter Pleads Guilty to Terrorism and Murder Charges in Racist Attack," CNN, November 28, 2022, https://edition.cnn.com/2022/11/28/us/buffalo-tops-grocery-shooting-payton-gendron-plea/index.html.
14. Y. W. Loke, "Placenta Spiritually Revered, But Not in the West," *Women's News*, July 28, 2013. https://womensenews.org/2013/07/placenta-spiritually-revered-not-in-the-west.
15. Sarah Hollister, *Placenta Burial Rituals*, accessed August 28, 2023, https://placentarisks.org/wp-content/uploads/2018/09/Placenta-burial-rituals-from-around-the-world-handout.pdf.
16. Hollister, *Placenta Burial Rituals*.